EUCHARIST: ENHANCING THE PRAYER

Donal Harrington

Eucharist: Enhancing the Prayer

including
Prayer of the Faithful for the Three Year Cycle

the columba press

First published in 2007 by
the columba press
55A Spruce Avenue, Stillorgan Industrial Park, Blackrock, Co Dublin

Cover by Bill Bolger
Origination by The Columba Press
Printed in Ireland by ColourBooks Ltd, Dublin

ISBN 978-1-85607-571-8

Table of Contents

Introduction

The overall aim of this book is to contribute to the quality of our prayer together when celebrating the Eucharist. People used to talk about the 'sense of mystery' at the old Latin Mass. Today also, we need a sense of 'something more', that connects us with divine presence. Creating an atmosphere of prayer, a prayerful mood, is part of this.

Much of it falls to the priest. There is a difference between 'saying Mass' and 'leading people in prayer', and there is a greater need today for leading people in prayer. For example, I am struck by how often the main statement at the start of Mass is: 'Today is the 17th Sunday in Ordinary Time'! Very simple and effective ways exist to move beyond this kind of routine, to create silence and space for prayer.

The idea in part one of this book is to make more of certain moments in the Mass as 'prayer moments'. There are seven in all – at the beginning, before the Liturgy of the Word, after the homily, at the presentation of the gifts, beginning the Eucharistic Prayer, at the Communion Rite, and before the final blessing.

At the each of these moments, there is a very brief, focused text, that is meant to invite people into a similarly brief moment of silence. I am not suggesting that all seven be highlighted in the same celebration – overdoing it could be its undoing! I do think there is great potential in having a few such moments in each celebration.

My hope is that, as well as helping people to enter into prayer, these texts will help develop appreciation for what is going on at the different points in the celebration. Hopefully, as parishes get used to the idea, they may be encouraged to compose their own texts.

Part two of the book contains sets of prayers of the faithful for the full three-year cycle, including sets for various feasts during the year and for various occasions in people's lives.

I know that, ideally, the prayers of the faithful would come from the faithful themselves. Even though this can be hard to achieve, there are little ideas – such as a prayer basket in the aisle – that help us in this direction. But, while acknowledging the local and the contextual, these prayers offer an additional focus.

Their concern is to transpose the message and meanings of the day's scripture into the mode of prayer. All the prayers here seek to echo the thought of the scripture readings, and they often use the phrases and vocabulary of the texts. They are imbued with what the scriptures are saying. Hopefully, this would be a help to people in taking the Word of God to heart.

I do not envisage that these sets of prayers would be used just as they are. I would see them being combined with prayers that can only be composed locally, according to what is topical and currently relevant. So I hope that people would select from these prayers (and reword them as they see fit), and include them with their own compositions.

I would like to suggest some further possibilities for these texts. One is that the prayers could be used to stimulate ideas for the homily. Usually it is the other way around, the subject-matter of the homily generating intercessions. But, since these prayers are coming out of the scriptures, it is also possible that they could suggest themes for preaching.

A further possibility is to use the texts in the context of scripture-based prayer, whether group or individual. To this end, an index is provided of all the scripture references for the three-year cycle. A prayer session can be built around a particular reading or set of readings. The intercessions could be used to complement or stimulate prayer from the group participants. And to start and end the session, one could draw on the texts for introducing and concluding the Mass.

Another possibility is created by the collation of all the prayers for the dead. This provides a considerable number of short intercessions to draw on at funerals or other prayer times around bereavement.

Much of the idea and encouragement for this book came from John O'Connell and Donal O'Doherty – two 'workers for the Kingdom' from the kingdom! With both gratitude and pleasure, I dedicate the book to them.

Beginning the Celebration

After the sign of the cross and the greeting,
one of the following may be used to create a spirit of quiet prayer.
Each text also includes a penitential rite.
At the end of this section there are some texts
for special times in the liturgical year.

(1)

There's a line in one of the psalms that provides a lovely start
for our Mass:
    'O gates lift high your heads
    You doors, be opened up
    and let the King of Glory enter in.'

Think of this as the gates and doors of your heart – and you're
inviting Christ to enter in …
    'O gates lift high your heads
    You doors, be opened up
    and let the King of Glory enter in.'

A few moments of quiet

Penitential prayer
And may we feel Christ's presence when he comes in…

Lord, you come into our hearts with forgiving love.
Lord have mercy.
Lord, you come into our gathering with uplifting joy.
Christ have mercy.
Lord, you come into our world with transforming power.
Lord have mercy.

(2)

We begin with a quiet moment. St Augustine said:
    'You have made us for yourself, O Lord
    and our hearts are restless
    until they rest in you.'

Quietly now, we feel God's rest in our restlessness ...

A few moments of quiet

Penitential prayer
And in the quiet, we feel the touch of God's compassion ...

In the stillness, Lord, speak words of forgiveness.
Lord have mercy.
In the stillness, Lord, calm our soul.
Christ have mercy.
In the stillness, Lord, guide our path to you.
Lord have mercy.

(3)

We begin by listening to what Jesus says:
   'Whoever comes to me will never be hungry
   Whoever believes in me will never be thirsty.'

Let us reflect for a moment – What am I hungering for? What am I thirsting for? And let us bring this to the Lord...

A few moments of quiet

Penitential prayer
We also bring to God our need for forgiving grace ...

With your mercy, Lord, we can move beyond past failures.
Lord have mercy.
With your mercy, Lord, we can make a new beginning.
Christ have mercy.
With your mercy, Lord, we can grow and flourish.
Lord have mercy.

(4)

We begin by listening to these words of Jesus:
    'Listen! I am standing at the door knocking.
    If you hear my voice and open the door
    I will come in to you and eat with you
    and you with me.'

And we take a moment to be quiet, to open the door of our heart, and ask the Lord in ...

A few moments of quiet

Penitential prayer
We ask the Lord to touch us with his mercy ...

Your mercy, Lord, warms our hearts.
Lord have mercy.
Your mercy, Lord, enlightens our minds.
Christ have mercy.
Your mercy, Lord, changes our lives.
Lord have mercy.

(5)

In the gospels, Jesus says that, if you fall out with one another, then first be reconciled to each other before coming to the altar.

So let's begin by quietly praying to be at peace with one another …

A few moments of quiet

Penitential prayer
Lord, you stay by our side when we find it hard to forgive.
Lord have mercy.
Lord, you hear our cry to be forgiven by those we hurt.
Christ have mercy.
Lord, your Spirit encourages us to be reconciled to one another.
Lord have mercy.

(6)

As we begin our Mass, we listen to Jesus speaking to us:
   'Ask and you will be given
   Knock and the door will be opened.'

We take a moment to be quiet – what is it that you ask of Jesus today? ...

A few moments of quiet

Penitential prayer
Included in what we ask, week in and week out, is to know God's forgiveness ...

May your forgiveness, Lord, heal us from doubting ourselves.
Lord have mercy.
May your mercy, Lord, restore our hope.
Christ have mercy.
May your kindness, Lord, release our love.
Lord have mercy.

(7)

At every Mass we say;
　　'Lord, I am not worthy… say the word and I shall be healed.'

Let's enter into a moment of quiet with that prayer.
　　Lord, I come before you in my need
　　and I come before you in my faith
　　that you can heal me.

A few moments of quiet

Penitential prayer

You heal us, Lord, and we believe that we are forgiven.
Lord have mercy.
You heal us, Lord, and we rejoice in our gifts.
Christ have mercy.
You heal us, Lord, so that we can find ourselves in giving
ourselves.
Lord have mercy.

(8)

We begin by listening to Jesus:
   'Where two or three are gathered in my name
   I am there with them.'

We have gathered here in Jesus' name. Let us take a moment to be quiet and become aware of him, present among us...

A few moments of quiet

Penitential prayer
And we pray for the consoling power of Christ's presence ...

Lord, your presence turns our minds to thoughts of good.
Lord have mercy.
Lord, your presence fills us with hope for living.
Christ have mercy.
Lord, your presence inspires us with love for others.
Lord have mercy.

(9)

We begin by listening to Jesus' invitation ...
    'If anyone loves me
    my Father will love them
    and we will come to them
    and make our home with them.'

We open the doors of our hearts ...
we invite Jesus in ...
we ask God to dwell in our hearts.

A few moments of quiet

Penitential prayer
And we open our hearts to God's forgiving love ...

Your love, Lord, reaches into every recess of our hearts.
Lord have mercy.
Your mercy, Lord, heals our past.
Christ have mercy.
Your compassion, Lord, restores our future.
Lord have mercy.

(10)

We begin with a quiet moment, listening to Jesus as he says ...
   'Come to me,
   all you who labour and are over-burdened
   and I will give you rest.'

We quietly share our cares with him.

A few moments of quiet

Penitential prayer
And we ask him to share his life with us ...

Lord, you lift our burden of sin.
Lord have mercy.
Lord, you give rest to our souls.
Christ have mercy.
Lord, you free us to follow you.
Lord have mercy.

(11)

We have a quiet moment at the start of Mass, thinking of what God wants each of us to be …

> Perhaps I am stronger than I think …
> Perhaps there is more to me than I want to see …
> Perhaps I am afraid of what I could be …
> Perhaps, O God, I am most afraid of your strength in me and prefer to stay small and weak in myself.

A few moments of quiet

Penitential prayer
May the Lord's mercy lift us up and transform us …

Lord, forgive us for feeling inadequate.
Lord have mercy.
Lord, forgive us for not trusting you.
Christ have mercy.
Lord, forgive us and make us strong.
Lord have mercy.

(12)

Beginning our Mass, we remember that it is God who gathers us and welcomes us here. We listen quietly as God speaks to us …

You have entered a place of warmth and safety.
You are welcome as you are;
there are no conditions.

You have entered a place of refuge and comfort.
You are welcome to unburden your soul.

You have entered a place of hope and longing.
You are welcome to let your spirit soar.

A few moments of quiet

Penitential prayer
And we pray to God who is all-forgiving …

Lord of warmth and safety, we welcome your embrace.
Lord have mercy.
Lord of refuge and comfort, we welcome your compassion.
Christ have mercy.
Lord of hope and longing, we welcome your call.
Lord have mercy.

(13)

I'll begin with a few words to help us be quiet in our hearts and minds...

> I weave a silence on my lips,
> I weave a silence into my mind,
> I weave a silence within my heart,
> I close my ears to distractions,
> I close my eyes to attentions,
> I close my heart to temptations.
> Calm me, O Lord, as you stilled the storm,
> Still me, O Lord, keep me from harm.
> Let all the tumult within me cease,
> Enfold me, Lord, in your peace.

A few moments of quiet

Penitential prayer
And in the quiet we allow ourselves feel the compassion of God...

Lord, you turn our minds to thoughts that are kind.
Lord have mercy.
Lord, you fill our hearts with love of one another.
Christ have mercy.
Lord, you open our lips to speak words of peace.
Lord have mercy.

(14)

Let us begin our Mass by stopping all the activity in our
minds, and becoming aware of God, with the help of these
words from Saint Teresa ...

> 'We need no wings to go in search of Him,
> but have only to find a place
> where we can be alone and look upon Him
> present within us.'

A few moments of quiet

Penitential prayer
In the stillness, we become aware of God looking upon us with
kindness ...

In your mercy, Lord, you forgive our sins.
Lord have mercy.
In your compassion, Lord, you blot out our guilt.
Christ have mercy.
In your love, Lord, you help us begin again.
Lord have mercy.

(15)

To prepare ourselves to celebrate the Eucharist, we take a pause to notice that God is present in us and among us...

O spring in the desert,
O shelter from the heat
O light in the darkness,
O guide for the feet
O joy in our sadness,
O support for the weak
O Lord with us always,
Your presence we seek.[1]

A few moments of quiet

Penitential prayer
May God now bring forgiveness wherever there is sin or guilt ...

Lord, you shelter us from harm.
Lord have mercy.
Lord, you guide us from darkness to light.
Christ have mercy.
Lord, you support us in our weakness.
Lord have mercy.

---

1. David Adam, *Tides and Seasons*, 122

(16)

I have a short prayer here, and with it I invite you to quietly
turn your heart and mind to God …

> Lord, you are my wealth and my strength;
> I bow before you.
> You are the giver of all the gifts that I have received,
> and of all the opportunities that lie ahead.
> Keep me, Lord, in your grace.

A few moments of quiet

Penitential prayer
And let us ask for the Lord's forgiving love …

You release us, Lord, from the guilt of our past.
Lord have mercy.
You free us, Lord, for the life that lies before us.
Christ have mercy.
You keep us, Lord, in your grace.
Lord have mercy.

(17)

As Mass begins, I invite you to become quiet, as we listen to this prayer...

As my soul grows quiet
I return to that amazing statement,
that at the heart of who I am
I am eternally loved –
Lord, I rest in your embrace.

A few moments of quiet

Penitential prayer
And we turn to the Lord and ask for forgiveness ...

Lord, your love conquers our fear.
Lord have mercy.
Lord, your mercy soothes our guilt.
Christ have mercy.
Lord, your call awakens our spirit.
Lord have mercy.

(18)

We begin with a prayer that asks us to bring everything to
God. And if we feel we have nothing to bring, then we bring
our nothing to God ...

> You must bring him everything!
> Your dreams, your successes, your rejoicing.
> And if you have little to rejoice over,
> bring him that little.
> And if your life seems only like
> a heap of fragments,
> bring him the fragments.
> And if you have only empty hands,
> bring him your empty hands.
> Shattered hopes are his material;
> in his hands all is made good.

A few moments of quiet

Penitential prayer
Lord, we ask for the power of your transforming love...

When sin makes us small, you make us great.
Lord have mercy.
When all we are is in fragments, you pull us together again.
Christ have mercy.
When we are empty, you fill us with hope.
Lord have mercy.

(19)

We have a moment of quiet prayer to begin our Mass. This prayer is about breathing in and breathing out – so I invite you to relax and follow the rhythm …

As we breathe in
we take in God's life that renews us
As we breathe out
we let out all that distracts us.

As we breathe in
we take in Jesus' strength that empowers us
As we breathe out
we let out all that oppresses us.

As we breathe in
we take in God's Spirit that frees us
As we breathe out
we let out all that closes us in on ourselves.

A few moments of quiet

Penitential prayer
And in the quiet we are able to hear God's healing voice …

Lord, you call us back when we get distracted.
Lord have mercy.
Lord, you give us strength when sin oppresses us.
Christ have mercy.
Lord, you open our hearts when we get closed in on ourselves.
Lord have mercy.

(20)

We begin our Mass with a moment of quiet ...

>We know, Lord, that you are closer to us
>than our own hearts.
>You are the heart of our being,
>the place of beauty within us.
>And silence puts us in touch with you.

A few moments of quiet

Penitential prayer
And we pray ...

You, O Lord, tell us who we are.
Lord have mercy.
You, O Lord, reassure us about ourselves.
Christ have mercy.
You, O Lord, call us to become what you see in us.
Lord have mercy.

(21)

As we begin Mass, we make a space for silence, and we tune ourselves in to God ...

> May your pace be our pace, O Lord;
> may our hearts beat with your heart;
> may your time be our time.

A few moments of quiet

Penitential prayer
And we ask God's forgiveness for our sins ...

Lord, you are the strength in our weakness.
Lord have mercy.
Lord, you are the encouragement in our failure.
Christ have mercy.
Lord, you are the healing in our brokenness.
Lord have mercy.

(22)

Let us begin our Mass by turning our eyes to God …

> We look on you, Lord,
> constant source of life,
> surprising source of blessing,
> irrepressible source of hope.

A few moments of quiet

Penitential prayer
As we look on you, Lord, we see your forgiving face…

Lord, you lead us to new life.
Lord have mercy.
Lord, you inspire us with your blessing.
Christ have mercy.
Lord, you are the hope of sinners.
Lord have mercy.

(23)

Often in the gospels, Jesus calls people by name – 'Mary',
'Peter', 'Martha', 'Andrew' – and it is a special moment.
So we are going to pause to think about each of us being called
by name …

> Think for a moment of your own name
> and let yourself hear Jesus speaking your name …

> You know how special your name sounds
> when said by special people who love you …

> So too, when Jesus says your name
> something special is happening.

A few moments of quiet

Penitential prayer
We now ask God to speak words of forgiveness to our hearts …

Lord, you call each of us by name.
Lord have mercy.
Lord, you lift us up when we fall.
Christ have mercy.
Lord, you ask us to reach beyond ourselves.
Lord have mercy.

(24)

At the start of our Mass, we open our hearts in silence, to hear a Word from God ...

> Listen to the Word – you are God's beloved.
> God lives within you,
> closer to you than your very self,
> assuring you that all is well.

A few moments of quiet

Penitential prayer
And now we await God's words of forgiveness ...

You are near us, Lord, when we fail.
Lord have mercy.
You are with us, Lord, when we repent.
Christ have mercy.
You are in us, Lord, when we change for the better.
Lord have mercy.

(25)

At the start of our Mass, we open our hearts in silence, to hear a Word from God …

> Listen to the Word – you are the Body of Christ.
> Christ's life flows through you
> and flows through us all,
> linking us together.

A few moments of quiet

Penitential prayer
And now we await God's words of forgiveness …

Lord, you call us to care for one another.
Lord have mercy.
Lord, you want us be at one with each other.
Christ have mercy.
Lord, you ask us to forgive one another.
Lord have mercy.

(26)

At the start of our Mass, we open our hearts in silence, to hear
a Word from God...

> Listen to the Word – God's Spirit is within you.
> Your spirit and God's Spirit are kindred spirits
> in tune with one another
> inspiring you
> helping you
> enthusing you.

A few moments of quiet

Penitential prayer
And now we await God's words of forgiveness ...

You inspire us, Lord, to begin again.
Lord have mercy.
You help us, Lord, in life's troubles.
Christ have mercy.
You enthuse us, Lord, with your Spirit.
Lord have mercy.

(27)

We begin by allowing ourselves a moment of quiet prayer and allowing ourselves to let go into God ...

Jesus, Lord, we let go into your arms;
Jesus, Lord, we let go into your plan;
Jesus, Lord, we let go into your power;
Jesus, Lord, we let go into your future.

A few moments of quiet

Penitential prayer
And we pray for God's forgiving grace ...

Lord, you help us to let go of our fear.
Lord have mercy.
Lord, you help us to let go of our guilt.
Christ have mercy.
Lord, you help us to let go of our smallness.
Lord have mercy.

(28)

As we start our Mass, we pray in silence – for silence is where
we find God … We stop and feel the silence that is God…

> We feel your presence, O listening God
> You who, in your infinite silence,
> hear far more than we can ever understand.

A few moments of quiet

Penitential prayer
And we pray …

Listening God, you hear our cries.
Lord have mercy.
Listening God, you dry our tears.
Christ have mercy.
Listening God, you console our spirit.
Lord have mercy.

(29)

I invite you to enter into a moment of quiet as we begin our
Mass …

> May there be peace in our hearts as we gather together.
> And in the peace of our hearts
> let us open our eyes
> to the presence and the wonder of God.

A few moments of quiet

Penitential prayer
We open our hearts to the wonder of God's mercy …

Merciful Lord, grace us with your peace.
Lord have mercy.
Merciful Lord, grace us with your confidence.
Christ have mercy.
Merciful Lord, grace us with your strength.
Lord have mercy.

(30)

To begin, I invite you to enter into the quiet of your heart,
where God will give you confidence.

May there be confidence in our hearts as we gather together.
Let us open our hearts to the Lord
and rely on the Lord's response.

A few moments of quiet

Penitential prayer
We open our hearts to hear God's words of compassion ...

Merciful Lord, bless us with your help.
Lord have mercy.
Merciful Lord, fill us with your confidence.
Christ have mercy.
Merciful Lord, grace us with your hope.
Lord have mercy.

(31)

To begin, I invite you to enter into the quiet of your heart,
where God will give you strength.

> May there be strength in our hearts as we gather together.
> May God's power build us up
> and make us eager for wholehearted giving.

A few moments of quiet

Penitential prayer
We open our hearts to be strengthened by God's mercy ...

Merciful Lord, build us up when we have sinned.
Lord have mercy.
Merciful Lord, build us up when we are weak.
Christ have mercy.
Merciful Lord, build us up for wholehearted giving.
Lord have mercy.

(32)

To begin, I invite you to enter into the quiet of your heart,
where God will give you hope.

> May there be hope in our hearts as we gather together.
> In courage may we let go of what holds us back
> and embrace God's call to be.

A few moments of quiet

Penitential prayer
We open our hearts to the hope that God's mercy offers ...

Merciful Lord, you are our hope when we have failed.
Lord have mercy.
Merciful Lord, you give us courage to move forward.
Christ have mercy.
Merciful Lord, you call forth the best in us.
Lord have mercy.

(33)

To begin, I invite you to enter into the quiet of your heart,
where God will give you enlightenment.

> May there be light in our hearts as we gather together.
> In the silence of our prayer may we listen
> and feel God's hand taking us on the right path.

A few moments of quiet

Penitential prayer
We open our hearts to be enlightened by God's mercy ...

Merciful Lord, you guide us on the right path.
Lord have mercy.
Merciful Lord, you are the light of our lives.
Christ have mercy.
Merciful Lord, you are our hope and salvation.
Lord have mercy.

(34)

The gospel tells us that we are forgiven people – at peace with
God. Let us give ourselves a moment for this truth to sink in
again …

>   We are forgiven.
>   We are loved.
>   We are blessed.

A few moments of quiet

Penitential prayer
And we pray in this spirit, celebrating God's forgiveness …

You, Lord, are the miracle of forgiving love.
Lord have mercy.
You, Lord, are the source of our peace.
Christ have mercy.
You, Lord, are the hope of our hearts.
Lord have mercy.

(35)

One of the psalms says:
'As a child has rest in its mother's arms, even so my soul.'

In that spirit, let us rest in God for a moment and quietly allow
God to embrace us ...
'As a child has rest in its mother's arms, even so my soul.'

A few moments of quiet

Penitential prayer
And let us feel forgiveness in God's embrace ...

Lord, in your loving arms we know forgiveness.
Lord have mercy.
Lord, in your loving arms we find peace.
Christ have mercy.
Lord, in your loving arms we feel new beginnings.
Lord have mercy.

(36)

We pray quietly for a moment. Younger or older, we are all growing, and now we connect in silence with God, who cares for our growth …

> Lord, I am like a seed,
> planted by you,
> full of hope,
> changing and growing.
> In the silence I recall
> how much you care for my growth.

A few moments of quiet

Penitential prayer
And we pray for the forgiveness that helps us to grow …

Lord, you soothe the fear that stops us growing.
Lord have mercy.
Lord, you heal the pride that stops us growing.
Christ have mercy.
Lord, you give us the confidence to grow and to change.
Lord have mercy.

(37)

One of the psalms says:
  'Be still and know that I am God.'

So let us begin our Mass with a still, quiet moment …

  Lord, let this present moment
  be as still as a stone
  as I rest my heart in you.

  All is still as a stone
  as I rest my heart in God.

A few moments of quiet

Penitential prayer
In the stillness, may we feel the peace of God's forgiving love …

Where spirits are anxious, calm us Lord with your peace.
Lord have mercy.
Where there is guilt or remorse, calm us Lord with your peace.
Christ have mercy.
Where hearts are restless, calm us Lord with your peace.
Lord have mercy.

(38)

We begin our worship together with a pause, to quieten ourselves and to make a space for God …

> Beloved Lord,
> breathe calm in my mind,
> peace in my heart,
> and silence in my soul.
> In the silence let me hear your voice,
> in the peace let me see your face,
> in the calm let me know your love.

A few moments of quiet

Penitential prayer
And now we ask that God's Spirit will rest on each of us and assure us of God's infinite compassion …

Speak to us, O Lord, in the silence of our souls.
Lord have mercy.
Show yourself to us, O Lord, in the peace of our hearts.
Christ have mercy.
Love us, O Lord, in the calm of our minds.
Lord have mercy.

(39)

We begin with a moment of quiet, connecting us to God and to the grace of this moment …

> The arms of God reach round us,
> we rest in their embrace;
> the heart of Jesus invites us,
> we look upon his face;
> the Spirit breathes upon us,
> welcome, this time of grace.

A few moments of quiet

Penitential prayer
And we ask for the forgiving face of God – Father, Son and Spirit – to look upon us …

Lord, your arms embrace us with infinite compassion.
Lord have mercy.
Lord, your heart is open, inviting us to share your life.
Christ have mercy.
Lord, your Spirit breathes on us with new life.
Lord have mercy.

(40)

To focus ourselves for this Mass, we quieten our minds and our hearts, and turn to God in quiet prayer ...

> God, our beginning and our end,
> God in all the times in our life,
> God you are our all, to you we turn.
> Create in our hearts this day
> a peace-filled silence as we pray.

A few moments of quiet

Penitential prayer
In this silence, we implore God's mercy ...

Lord, in this silence we feel your forgiveness.
Lord have mercy.
Lord, in this silence we hear your call.
Christ have mercy.
Lord, in this silence we cling to your love.
Lord have mercy.

(41)

We begin with a thought from Saint Columcille, to help us tio
be quiet and to listen for God …

> Sometimes in a lonely cell
> in the presence of my God
> I stand and listen.
> In the silence of my heart
> I can hear God's will
> when I listen.
> For I am but a servant
> who is guided by my king
> when I listen.

A few moments of quiet

Penitential prayer
As we listen, we hear God's healing, consoling voice …

Lord, fill the silence in our hearts with your mercy.
Lord have mercy.
Lord, fill the silence in our hearts with your peace.
Christ have mercy.
Lord, fill the silence in our hearts with your energy.
Lord have mercy.

(42) *Advent*

Advent is a time of longing. We link in to its spirit of
expectation now with a moment of quiet

> There is a longing in our hearts
> which Christ comes to fulfil.
> Come, Lord, into our open hearts
> and welcome you we will.

A few moments of quiet

Penitential prayer
May Christ enter our hearts with forgiving love …

Lord, you feed us in our hunger.
Lord have mercy.
Lord, you satisfy our thirst.
Christ have mercy.
Lord, you meet us in our longing.
Lord have mercy.

(43) *Advent*

In this Advent time, we ask the Lord to come into the quiet of
our hearts …

> Come Lord, come down,
> Come in, come among us.
> Come as the wind to move us,
> Come as the light to prove us,
> Come as the night to rest us,
> Come as the storm to test us,
> Come as the sun to warm us,
> Come as the stillness to calm us,
> Come Lord, come down,
> Come in, come among us.[2]

A few moments of quiet

Penitential prayer
May the Lord come with forgiveness into our hearts …

The Lord comes with loving mercy to warm us.
Lord have mercy.
The Lord comes with peace to calm us.
Christ have mercy.
The Lord comes with life to invigorate us.
Lord have mercy.

---

2. David Adam, *Tides and Seasons*, 22.

(44) *Advent/Christmas*

As we begin, listen to these strange words from Meister
Eckhart, a mystic from many centuries ago ...
'We are all meant to be mothers of God
because God is always needing to be born.'

And let's be quiet for a moment – something new being born
in me – new life, new hope, from deep within, where God is ...
'We are all meant to be mothers of God
because God is always needing to be born.'

A few moments of quiet

Penitential prayer
And we pray ...

Lord, your birth is light in our confusion.
Lord have mercy.
Lord, your birth is joy in our gloom.
Christ have mercy.
Lord, your birth is a new beginning in our failure.
Lord have mercy.

(45) *Christmas*

'The Word became flesh and dwelt among us.'

Let's pause for a moment to let the mystery of Christmas sink in…

God has come close…
God makes a home in our hearts…
We are embraced in an unbelievable love…

A few moments of quiet

Penitential prayer
And may the assurance of God's forgiveness dwell in our hearts …

Word made flesh, shine light in our darkness.
Lord have mercy.
Word made flesh, live in our hearts.
Christ have mercy.
Word made flesh, be born in our lives.
Lord have mercy.

(46) *Baptism*

We begin our Mass with a quiet moment, thinking of who we
are as Christians …

> If you forget your roots and where you came from
> you forget who you are.
> If you remember your roots
> you stay in touch with who you are.

> Today we remember where we came from – our baptism
> when we became members of the Christian family –
> we rejoice in our dignity as children of God,
> as brothers and sisters of Jesus Christ,
> as bearers of the Holy Spirit in the world.

A few moments of quiet

Sprinkling
As I sprinkle you with the water of baptism
may you ever carry in your mind
the knowledge of who you are –
and ever carry into your living
the challenge of who you are called to be.

(47) *Baptism*

To begin our Mass, we pause to reflect on the fact that we are
baptised. These words of Pope John Paul say something about
what it means:
> At their baptism,
> every Christian hears again the voice that was once heard
> speaking to Jesus on the banks of the Jordan river:
> 'You are my beloved;
> with you I am well pleased.'

Allow these words to impact on you. Be quiet and listen to
God saying again what God first said to us at our baptism:
> 'You are my beloved.'

A few moments of quiet

Penitential prayer
We ask now that God's love would heal us and bring us
strength …

You came to tell us of God's love.
Lord have mercy.
You forgive us when we fail to love.
Christ have mercy.
You challenge us to increase the love in the world.
Lord have mercy.

(48) *Lent*

We begin quietly, making ourselves still and opening ourselves
to the meaning of Lent …

> Lent means days are lengthening;
> brightness is returning;
> new growth is all around us.

> Lent is my heart's journey when I fast –
> letting go of what is false,
> I listen to the Lord of life
> calling me to live
> like I never lived before.

A few moments of quiet

Penitential prayer
And we open ourselves to the power of God's mercy …

You call us to love you with all our heart.
Lord have mercy.
You call us to love you with all our soul.
Christ have mercy.
You call us to love you with all our strength.
Lord have mercy.

(49) *Lent/Transfiguration*

In today's gospel, Peter says to Jesus, 'It is wonderful to be
here.' So let us now – all of us, here – be quiet of a moment
and think the same thought, 'It is wonderful to be here' ...

> It is wonderful to be with you, O God,
> to share this time,
> to be in this space,
> to know this grace.

A few moments of quiet

Penitential prayer
And we pray for the transforming power of your forgiveness ...

Your glory, Lord, shines light into our minds.
Lord have mercy.
Your glory, Lord, pours love into our hearts.
Christ have mercy.
Your glory, Lord, bestows peace in the silence.
Lord have mercy.

(50) *Palm Sunday*

We begin our Mass, and we begin our week – our Holy Week –
with a moment of quiet, listening to a lovely old Irish prayer,
that asks Jesus in his passion to touch us this week, to heal us
and to bring us life …

> O King of the Friday
> whose limbs were stretched on the cross;
> O Lord who did suffer
> the bruises, the wounds and the loss;
> we stretch ourselves
> beneath the shield of your might;
> some fruit from the tree of your passion
> fall on us this night.

A few moments of quiet

Penitential prayer
We open ourselves to the power of Christ's passion …

Lord, your passion touches us in our pain.
Lord have mercy.
Lord, your passion heals us and makes us whole.
Christ have mercy.
Lord, your passion brings life where there was death.
Lord have mercy.

(51) *Easter*

To begin our Mass, we stay quiet for a moment, to let ourselves touch into the spirit of hope, so alive in this Easter season ...

> May Easter mean for me
> new beginnings,
> fresh ways of seeing,
> new reason to hope.

A few moments of quiet

Penitential prayer
We call now on the mercy and compassion of the risen Lord ...

Lord Jesus, risen from the dead, you inspire us to begin again.
Lord have mercy.
Lord Jesus, risen from the dead, you encourage us to see things differently.
Christ have mercy.
Lord Jesus, risen from the dead, you give us reason to hope.
Lord have mercy.

(52) *Easter*

We begin our Mass today with a blessing with Easter water.
Just before the blessing, a moment's meditation...

Think of a plant that is languishing, thirsting,
needing nourishment;
and think of it being watered
and coming to life again,
from the roots and up each branch.

And think of yourself this Easter.
Feel the new life of Easter running up through you,
with the refreshment your spirit craves,
with the energy your soul has been aching for.

A few moments of quiet

I will bless you now with the Easter water,
and as I do,
allow the grace of Easter to work in you.

Sprinkling with Easter water

(53) *Spirit*

To begin Mass today, think for a moment about God's Spirit –
the Spirit of Jesus – and what the Spirit can do for us …
    Grant us extraordinary grace,
    O Spirit hidden in the dark in us and deep
    and bring to light the dream out of our sleep.

Be quiet and feel God's Spirit stirring within you, daring you
to believe, daring you to dream …
    Grant us extraordinary grace,
    O Spirit hidden in the dark in us and deep
    and bring to light the dream out of our sleep.

A moment of quiet

Penitential prayer
And we ask for the Spirit's healing, life-giving power …

Lord, your Spirit is our source of life, deep within our hearts.
Lord have mercy.
Lord, your Spirit within connects us to you and your dream.
Christ have mercy.
Lord, your Spirit brings to light the dream out of our sleep.
Lord have mercy.

(54) *Spirit*

Our quiet moment today is about what it means to receive the Holy Spirit. Listen to what Saint Paul says:
'We have received the Spirit that is from God
so that we may understand
the gifts that God bestows on us.'

The Spirit lives in me ... The Spirit tells me that I am gifted by God ... With the eyes of my heart, I look on myself as God's Spirit sees me.

A moment of quiet

Penitential prayer
And we ask for the Spirit's healing, life-giving power ...

Lord, your healing Spirit meets us in our failure.
Lord have mercy.
Lord, your Spirit shows us how gifted we are.
Christ have mercy.
Lord, with your Spirit, we can be a gift to one another.
Lord have mercy.

Before the Liturgy of the Word

Just before the Liturgy of the Word, to focus attention,
the priest says one of the following texts.
The quotations are all taken from the psalms.

(1)
We listen now to the Word of God and we pray ...
    'My soul waits for your word, O Lord,
    and in your word I hope.'

brief pause

(2)
Let us pause for a moment and open our hearts to God's Word ...
    'Let the light of your face shine on us O Lord.'

brief pause

(3)
We prepare quietly to hear God's Word today ...
    'You, Lord, will show me the path of life.'

brief pause

(4)
Now God is going to speak; let us quieten our hearts ...
    'You, O Lord, are my lamp; you lighten my darkness.'

brief pause

(5)
Before the Word of God, we stop and pray ...
    'You guide us, O Lord, along the right path.'

brief pause

(6)
Let us make ourselves ready for what God is saying to us
today ...
    'Open the door of your heart, that the Lord may enter in.'

brief pause

(7)

We pause before we listen to God's Word ...
  'Lord, make me know your ways, teach me your paths.'

brief pause

(8)

Now we listen to God; may this be a moment of grace ...
  'Make me walk in your ways and teach me,
  for you are my God.'

brief pause

(9)

We open our ears and open our hearts to the Word of God ...
  'By your word, O Lord,
  show us the path we should choose.'

brief pause

(10)

We listen now to the Word of God and we pray ...
  'The Lord is my light and my help.'

brief pause

(11)

Let us pause for a moment and open our hearts to God's Word ...
  'It is your face, O Lord, that I seek; hide not your face.'

brief pause

(12)

We prepare quietly to hear God's Word today ...
  'Lord, instruct us, and teach us the way we should go.'

brief pause

(13)
Now God is going to speak; let us quieten our hearts ...
'Our soul is waiting for you, O Lord; we trust in your word.'

brief pause

(14)
Before the Word of God, we stop and pray ...
'May your love be upon us, O Lord,
as we place all our hope in you.'

brief pause

(15)
Let us make ourselves ready for what God is saying to us
today ...
'In you, O Lord, is the source of life,
and in your light we see light.'

brief pause

(16)
We pause before we listen to God's Word ...
'We count on you, O Lord; it is you who will answer.'

brief pause

(17)
Now we listen to God; may this be a moment of grace ...
'My soul is thirsting for God, the God of my life.'

brief pause

(18)

We open our ears and open our hearts to the Word of God …
 'Send forth your light and your truth, let these be my guide.'

brief pause

(19)

We listen now to the Word of God and we pray …
 'We praise your word, O God; in you we trust.'

brief pause

(20)

Let us pause for a moment and open our hearts to God's Word …
 'O God you are my God, for you I long;
 for you my soul is thirsting.'

brief pause

(21)

We prepare quietly to hear God's Word today …
 'Give heed, my people, to my teaching;
 turn your ear to the words of my mouth.'

brief pause

(22)

Now God is going to speak; let us quieten our hearts …
 'I will hear what the Lord has to say,
 a voice that speaks of peace.'

brief pause

(23)

Before the Word of God, we stop and pray ...

'Show me, Lord, your way so that I may walk in your truth.'

brief pause

(24)

Let us make ourselves ready for what God is saying to us today...

'Lord, send forth your word to heal us.'

brief pause

(25)

We pause before we listen to God's Word ...

'I will ponder all your teachings; I will not forget your word.'

brief pause

(26)

Now we listen to God; may this be a moment of grace ...

'Open my eyes that I may see the wonders of your law.'

brief pause

(27)

We open our ears and open our hearts to the Word of God ...

'Keep me from the way of error and teach me your law.'

brief pause

(28)

We listen now to the Word of God and we pray ...

'Your word gives freedom to my heart.'

brief pause

(29)

We pause for a moment and open our hearts to God's Word ...
'Guide me in the path of your commands,
for there is my delight.'

brief pause

(30)

We prepare quietly to hear God's Word today ...
'Keep my eyes from what is false;
by your word give me life.'

brief pause

(31)

Now God is going to speak; let us quieten our hearts ...
'Lord, your love fills the earth; teach me your truth.'

brief pause

(32)

Before the Word of God, we stop and pray ...
'The words from your mouth mean more to me
than silver and gold.'

brief pause

(33)

Let us make ourselves ready for what God is saying to us
today ...
'Let your love come and I shall live;
for your word is my delight.'

brief pause

(34)
We pause before we listen to God's Word ...
   'I yearn for your saving help; I hope in your word.'

brief pause

(35)
Now we listen to God; may this be a moment of grace ...
   'Your word is a lamp for my steps and a light for my path.'

brief pause

(36)
We open our ears and open our hearts to the Word of God ...
   'You are my shelter, my shield; I hope in your word.'

brief pause

(37)
We listen now to the Word of God and we pray ...
   'I am your servant; give me knowledge;
   then I will know your will.'

brief pause

(38)
Let us pause for a moment and open our hearts to God's Word ...
   'Let your face shine on your servant;
   teach me your decrees.'

brief pause

(39)

We prepare quietly to hear God's Word today …
  'My heart is listening; if you teach me I shall live.'

brief pause

(40)

Now God is going to speak; let us quieten our hearts …
  'I rise before dawn and cry for help; I hope in your word.'

brief pause

(41)

Before the Word of God, we stop and pray …
  'In your love hear my voice, O Lord;
  give me life by your word.'

brief pause

(42)

Let us make ourselves ready for what God is saying to us
today …
  'Lord, let my cry come before you; teach me by your word.'

brief pause

(43)

We pause before we listen to God's Word …
  'My help shall come from the Lord,
  who made heaven and earth.'

brief pause

(44)

Now we listen to God; may this be a moment of grace …
    'Out of the depths I cry to you, O Lord.
    My soul is waiting for you; I count on your word.'

brief pause

(45)

We open our ears and open our hearts to the Word of God …
    'To you, Lord God, my ears are turned,
    to hear your word of life.'

brief pause

(46)

We listen now to the Word of God and we pray …
    'Make me know the way I should walk,
    for I put my trust in you.'

brief pause

(47)

Let us pause for a moment and open our hearts to God's Word …
    'Instruct me, Lord, by your word;
    let your good Spirit guide me.'

brief pause

(48)

We prepare quietly to hear God's Word today …
    'O that today we would listen to your voice, O Lord.'

brief pause

After the Homily

*At the end of the homily, to facilitate quiet reflection,
the priest says one of the following.*

(1)

We pause for a moment in quiet,
to allow the Word of God to sink into our hearts today …

followed by quiet moment

(2)

And now, let's pause – you've been listening to me – together
we have listened to God's Word. Quietly for a moment – what
is God saying to you today? …

followed by quiet moment

(3)

Let's stop for a moment and ask – what do I hear God saying
to me today? …

followed by quiet moment

(4)

We'll pause now for a moment to focus on what we hear the
Lord saying to us today …

followed by quiet moment

(5)

We've listened to God's Word – you've listened to me – now
quietly, listen to your heart – what do I hear from God today? …

followed by quiet moment

(6)

Now, let us quieten our minds and thoughts for a moment, to
hear the message that God has for us today …

followed by quiet moment

(7)

Let's pause for a moment to let the words of today's Mass sink into our hearts …

followed by quiet moment

(8)

I invite you now to ask yourself, in silence – from what you have heard today, what finds an echo in your heart? …

followed by quiet moment

(9)

We've been listening for a while – so now, in the silence of your heart, tell God what you have been hearing in our Mass today…

followed by quiet moment

(10)

We now have a moment's quiet, to absorb what we have heard today, in the readings and the homily …

followed by quiet moment

(11)

Before moving on, we'll have a quiet moment to think: what is the Lord saying to me today? …

followed by quiet moment

(12)

I've been talking about the Word of God which we have listened to. Now I invite you to talk quietly within yourself, about what you hear God saying today …

followed by quiet moment

At the Presentation of the Gifts

As an aid to appreciating the meaning
of this part of the celebration,
one of the following reflections could be spoken
by the priest or a member of the assembly,
as the gifts are being presented.

(1)
As you see bread and wine being brought
to the table of the Lord
do not see only bread and wine
but also see yourselves
represented in these gifts.

You are included in what is being presented.
Allow yourself to be placed on the altar –
to be part of what is transformed
into the Body of Christ.

brief moment of quiet

(2)
As we prepare the altar, we ask ourselves –
what are we bringing to the Lord's table?

Bread and wine, yes –
but also ourselves.

We belong on the table of the Lord
ready to be changed
into the Body of Christ.

brief moment of quiet

(3)

One of the hymns we sing at this time of Mass says;
'In bread we bring you, Lord, our bodies' labour,
in wine we offer you our spirits' grief.'

We bring to the altar our sweat and struggle,
our joy and laughter,
our tears and tensions,
our hopes and needs,
our hearts and souls – ourselves.
brief moment of quiet

(4)

The bread we bring is made from many grains
to become one bread.
The wine we bring is the juice
of many grapes.
So we, who are many,
are now being gathered into one –
the one Body of Christ.

brief moment of quiet

(5)

We bring bread and wine to the altar.
Bread and wine signify fellowship –
meals together, breaking bread, sharing our lives.

Today they mean the Body of Christ –
our fellowship as members of his body,
broken for us –
He shares life with us,
which we will share in turn.

brief moment of quiet

(6)
Some people come to Mass
and leave their lives outside the door.
Now is the time to pick up your life
and join it with the bread and wine
being brought to the Lord's table.

Pick up your life –
your worries and wishes,
your relationships, your reality –
and place it on the altar.
Your gift – your self –
your prayer.

brief moment of quiet

(7)
As bread and wine are brought to the table of the Lord,
we remind ourselves
that we are not spectators.
We are not here to watch something.
We are here to do something –
together.
We are all here to *participate* in this sacred action.

brief moment of quiet

(8)
Bread and wine are brought to the altar.
There are many for whom bread is a luxury,
not to mention wine.
For us, they are signs of plenty –
of how much we possess
in being loved by God.

And they are signs of how much we must give,
to make life better for everybody.

brief moment of quiet

(9)
Besides bread and wine,
we also bring forward our collection for [*name the cause*].
This collection expresses our belief in Jesus' calling –
to wash each other's feet, to serve each other.

In the Eucharist, Jesus humbly washes our feet.
May we allow him to do so,
and may we serve each other in turn.

brief moment of quiet

(10)
As far as we know, at the Last Supper,
all that Jesus had on the table was bread and wine.
Through these he signified
that he was giving himself.

Today we place bread and wine on our table,
the table of the Lord.
In doing so, we signify
that we are giving ourselves –
to be one with him
who gives himself to us.

brief moment of quiet

(11)
The gifts of bread and wine are now being brought forward
to be presented at the altar.
As our eyes watch, and look at the bread and wine,
we let our hearts join in the movement to the altar.
We join ourselves with the bread and wine –
for we too must approach the altar of the Lord.

brief moment of quiet

(12)
Something to reflect on as the gifts of bread and wine
are brought to the altar ...

Jesus' life revolved around bread and wine –
sitting at table with all kinds of people,
sharing table, sharing lives – restoring hope,
bringing the smile back to their faces.
May it be so for us, today.

brief moment of quiet

(13)
The gifts of bread and wine are now brought forward.
The people carrying them won't stop at the step of the sanctuary,
but will place them on the altar themselves.
This is a way of saying that this altar is our table
and that we belong there –
we who are the Body of Christ.

brief moment of quiet

(14) *When using Eucharistic Prayer III*
A thought as we bring gifts of bread and wine to the altar ...

In our Eucharist Prayer we say:
  'We ask you to make them holy by the power of your Spirit,
  that *they* may become the body and blood of your Son.'

And then we say:
  'Grant that *we* may be filled with the Holy Spirit
  and become one body, one spirit in Christ'.

Bread and wine become the body and blood of Christ;
we too are changed; we become Christ's Body.

brief moment of quiet

(15)
The bread and wine are carried up the church to the altar.
They come from among us who are gathered here.
The bread and wine represent us –
ourselves and all our lives ...
We present ourselves at the table of the Lord –
to be transformed.

brief moment of quiet

87

(16)

As the bread and wine are brought to the altar
we listen to these words of Saint Augustine,
speaking of the wine:
    'Remember how wine is made.
    Many grapes hang from the vine,
    but all the juice flows into one.
    And that is what Jesus Christ means to us.
    He wants us to belong in him,
    to pour into him as one.
    It is the mystery of our peace and unity
    which he consecrates on his table'.

brief moment of quiet

(17)

As bread and wine are presented at the altar,
think for a moment about the bread and what it means ...
Bread is made from many grains,
baked together to become one bread.
We too are many and we are gathered together as one,
the one Body of Christ.
One bread – one body.

brief moment of quiet

At the Eucharistic Prayer

To facilitate active participation in this part of the celebration,
the priest says one of the following reflections,
just after the prayer over the gifts
and just before 'The Lord be with you'.

(1)
We now begin the Eucharistic Prayer –
a prayer of giving thanks.

Just pause for a moment to think;
What am I thankful for?

And bring that to God.

very brief pause before continuing

(2)
The Eucharistic Prayer is our great prayer of thanks to God.
Since it is our prayer
you might like to speak its words in your heart
as I speak in the name of all of us gathered here.

very brief pause before continuing

(3)
In the Liturgy of the Word
God has been speaking to us.

Now, in this Eucharistic Prayer,
God is silent –
listening to our words,
spoken by me on behalf of us all.

very brief pause before continuing

(4)
We begin our great prayer of thanks –
'thanks' is what 'Eucharist' means.

May God feel our thanksgiving
coming through in this prayer.

very brief pause before continuing

(5)
In the Eucharistic Prayer –
We look back in thanks
remembering Jesus' Last Supper.
We look forward with hope
in God's promises.
We look around in awareness –
Jesus in our midst.

very brief pause before continuing

(6)
This is the time in the Mass
when we speak to God
with hearts full of thanks and praise.

So, let our prayer flow freely from our hearts.

very brief pause before continuing

(7)
As we begin the Eucharistic Prayer
we hear the words, 'Lift up your hearts.'

May each one here feel their spirits uplifted,
as we remember the story
of God's life given to us.

very brief pause before continuing

(8)
Now, in the Eucharistic Prayer,
we join our hearts together in thanking God
for the gift of Jesus –
Jesus, who now joins us together in him,
the Body of Christ.

very brief pause before continuing

(9)
In times past, people prayed quietly on their own
for this part of the Mass.
But today it is a 'together' time, not a private time –
and the Eucharistic Prayer is our prayer together.

As I say the words
It is we – all of us – praying.

very brief pause before continuing

(10)
We now begin the Eucharistic Prayer.
We give thanks to God for many things –
for ourselves –
for one another –
for life –
for whatever is in your heart just now.

And we give thanks for Christ,
the gift of God's life.

very brief pause before continuing

(11)
As we begin the Eucharistic Prayer,
let's remember that we are not here on our own,
in an 'individual capacity'.
We may not all know each other,
but we are together as one.

And this is our 'together prayer'
in which we are deeply one –
the Body of Christ.

very brief pause before continuing

(12)
A few minutes ago our eyes were directed
to the table of the Word
as we listened to the scriptures.

Now our eyes are focused on this table,
the table of the Eucharist.
What our many eyes can see – one bread and one cup,
What our many hearts can know – we are one body.

In this Spirit we pray.

very brief pause before continuing

(13)
In the Eucharistic Prayer we will remember
what God has done for us.

We will ask the Spirit to transform these gifts –
and to transform us –
into the Body of Christ.

very brief pause before continuing

(14)
In a moment you will hear the words,
'Let us give thanks to the Lord our God'.

We give thanks for life itself
and for the grace we experience in so many ways.

We give thanks to the giver of these gifts.

very brief pause before continuing

(15) *with Eucharistic Prayer I*
In a moment you will hear the words,
'We come to you Father with praise and thanksgiving.'

This is our great prayer of thanks
when we leave aside all other thoughts
and just rejoice in what God has done for us in Christ.

very brief pause before continuing

(16) *with Eucharistic Prayer II*
In a moment you will hear the words,
'It is our duty and salvation always and everywhere to give
you thanks.'

This is our great prayer of thanks
when we leave aside all other thoughts
and just rejoice in what God has done for us in Christ.

very brief pause before continuing

(17) *with Eucharistic Prayer III*
In a moment you will hear the words,
'You are holy indeed and all creation rightly gives you praise.'

This is our great prayer of thanks
when we leave aside all other thoughts
and just rejoice in what God has done for us in Christ.

very brief pause before continuing

(18) *with Eucharistic Prayer IV*
In a moment you will hear the words,
'Father in heaven it is right that we should give you thanks
and praise'.

This is our great prayer of thanks
when we leave aside all other thoughts
and just rejoice in what God has done for us in Christ.

very brief pause before continuing

(19) *with Eucharistic Prayer for Children I*
In a moment you will hear the words,
'God our Father, you have brought us here together
so that we can give you thanks and praise
for all the wonderful things you have done.'

This is our big prayer of thanks
when we say 'Thank you God for everything.'

very brief pause before continuing

(20) *with Eucharistic Prayer for Children II*
In a moment you will hear the words,
'God, our loving Father, we are glad to give you thanks and
praise'.

This is our big prayer of thanks
when we say 'Thank you God for everything.'

very brief pause before continuing

(21) *with Eucharistic Prayer for Children III*
In a moment you will hear the words,
'We thank you, God our Father.'

This is our big prayer of thanks
when we say 'Thank you God for everything.'

very brief pause before continuing

(22) *with Eucharistic Prayer for Reconciliation I*
In a moment you will hear the words,
'We do well always and everywhere to give you thanks.'

This is our great prayer of thanks;
we leave aside all other thoughts
and just rejoice at what God has done in Christ.

very brief pause before continuing

(23) *with Eucharistic Prayer for Reconciliation II*
In a moment you will hear the words,
'Father, we praise and thank you.'

This is our great prayer of thanks;
we leave aside all other thoughts
and just rejoice at what God has done in Christ.

very brief pause before continuing

(24) *with Eucharistic Prayer, 'The Church on the Way to Unity'*
In a moment you will hear the words,
'It is truly right to give you thanks.'

This is our great prayer of thanks
when we leave aside all other thoughts
and just rejoice in what God has done for us in Christ.

very brief pause before continuing

(25) *with Eucharistic Prayer, 'God Guides the Church on the Way of
      Salvation'*
In a moment you will hear the words,
'It is truly right and just always and everywhere to give you
thanks.'

This is our great prayer of thanks
when we leave aside all other thoughts
and just rejoice in what God has done for us in Christ.

very brief pause before continuing

(26) *with Eucharistic Prayer, 'Jesus, Way to the Father'*
In a moment you will hear the words,
'It is truly right and just always and everywhere to give you
thanks.'

. This is our great prayer of thanks
when we leave aside all other thoughts
and just rejoice in what God has done for us in Christ.

very brief pause before continuing

(27) *with Eucharistic Prayer, 'Jesus, the Compassion of God'*
In a moment you will hear the words,
'It is truly right to give you thanks.'

This is our great prayer of thanks
when we leave aside all other thoughts
and just rejoice in what God has done for us in Christ.

very brief pause before continuing

At the Communion Rite

*One of the following could be used as an introduction
to the Our Father and the Communion Rite.*

(1)
This Eucharist makes us into one family
with one Father, the God of our Lord Jesus Christ.

We pray in a spirit of unity;

Our Father …

(2)
We say together the prayer
that is above all prayers
because it is the prayer Jesus taught us;

Our Father …

(3)
We are now beginning the Communion part of Mass.
We are gathered here as a family and we pray as a family;

Our Father …

(4)
God did not call us, each on our own.
God called us to be a family.
That we may be what God wants us to be,
we pray;

Our Father …

(5)
Our most precious prayer must surely be
the one that Jesus gave us.
So we pray it now, savouring its words;

Our Father …

AT THE COMMUNION RITE

(6)
Our lives are one great search
for the face of the One who created us
and who loves us with an everlasting love.
We pray together;

Our Father ...

(7)
Our next prayer joins us with Christians
of all denominations
throughout the world.
As one great family, we pray;

Our Father ...

(8)
Jesus told us that we have one Father in heaven
and that we are all God's children.
Let us pray with a bond of unity between us;

Our Father ...

(9)
There is unity between us
because we are all focused on God.
We have a common bond,
and the prayer we now say
is our shared prayer,
spoken with one heart and mind.

Our Father ...

(10)
Our hearts will be restless
until they rest in God –
God is our hearts' desire
and we pray;

Our Father …

(11)
The Our Father is our prayer as a Christian family
and I now invite everybody to join hands
as we pray together;

Our Father …

(12)
Our Lord Jesus Christ wants us to feel confident –
to be confident human beings.
That is why he taught us to say this prayer together;

Our Father …

Sending Thoughts

The purpose of these thoughts is
to engender a feeling of 'being sent'
as the Eucharist comes to a conclusion.
After the prayer after communion,
the priest says one of the following reflections,
just after 'The Lord be with you'
and just before the final blessing.

(1)

Now, a blessing prayer, to send us on our way ...

> Deep peace of the running wave to you
> deep peace of the flowing air to you
> deep peace of Christ, the light of the world to you.[1]

> As you go, let this peace radiate from you.

pause, followed by blessing and dismissal

(2)

We have prayed together; now we are sent on our mission ...

> The love of God flowing free
> The love of God flow out through me.
> The peace of God flowing free
> The peace of God flow out through me.
> The life of God flowing free
> The life of God flow out through me.

pause, followed by blessing and dismissal

(3)

As we go, a thought for the road ...

> Listen
> be gentle
> take pleasure
> in the wonder
> and the beauty of the earth.
> Speak your love.

pause, followed by blessing and dismissal

---

1. Iona Community, adapted.

(4)

This is the moment when we are sent with a mission…

> Lord, you are love,
> we bring your love from here;
> Lord, you are compassion,
> we bring your compassion from here;
> Lord, you are gentle,
> we bring your gentleness from here.

pause, followed by blessing and dismissal

(5)

Now, we have a sacred moment of sending …

> Lord, we look back with thanks on all you have done for us.
> We look forward in hope for all you promise us.
> We look around in awareness to hear your call.

pause, followed by blessing and dismissal

(6)

As we go from here to do God's work, we ask God's blessing …

> Lord, shine light on our path;
> put hope in our heart;
> bring fruit to our work.

pause, followed by blessing and dismissal

(7)

As part of the blessing, a prayer 'sending' us on our mission …

> We leave here today, O Lord,
> with a new feeling of your presence.
> May we bring your Spirit with us
> and make a difference to others
> by the way we live.

pause, followed by blessing and dismissal

(8)

We go from here to live the Christian life…

> Lord, may we feel your power.
> May we know your hope.
> May we rise to your challenge.
> May we radiate your joy.

pause, followed by blessing and dismissal

(9)

And now, Lord, we ask you to bless us on our way …

> Lord, your Spirit has renewed our spirit.
> Protect us from losing heart;
> sustain our enthusiasm;
> may we radiate hope.

pause, followed by blessing and dismissal

(10)

Let us pray for God's blessing as we go to live God's life …

> God of new beginnings, lead us forward this day.
> God who abides within us,
> be revealed to all we meet this day.
> God who consoles and protects us,
> help us soothe any heartache this day.

pause, followed by blessing and dismissal

(11)

We ask God's blessing to guide us as we go from here …

> Bless us, O Lord, in our work today,
> bless us, O Lord, and be with us, we pray.
> May all that we do your glory proclaim,
> may all that we do be done in your name.

pause, followed by blessing and dismissal

(12)

God now sends us from here, so we ask a blessing …

For the Eucharist, which is the heart of our lives
and which is the heart of the world,
we give thanks to you, O Lord.
That we may live it in our lives
for the good of the world,
we pray to you, O Lord.

pause, followed by blessing and dismissal

(13)

Now, the Lord sends us on our way, to live the message of this
Eucharist …

Lord, you go before us at every moment.
You are in every person we meet
and in every experience we have.
Give us the gift of awareness
with eyes to see
and hearts to love.

pause, followed by blessing and dismissal

(14)

We go now to translate our prayer into action …

Lord, teach us to love well
and to overcome the obstacles in our own hearts.
May our love show to others
something of your boundless and inclusive love.
May it increase the peace in the world.

pause, followed by blessing and dismissal

(15)
God now sends us from here to make a difference in the world ...

Spirit of new life,
make us feel confident about our gifts
and help us appreciate the gifts of others.

pause, followed by blessing and dismissal

(16)
We have prayed together; now we are sent on our mission ...

Lord of our salvation,
inspire in us a spirit of service
as we dedicate ourselves
to the good of one another.

pause, followed by blessing and dismissal

(17)
We have received love; now we are sent to give love ...

God our creator,
release love's energy in our hearts
and make it real and active in our lives.

pause, followed by blessing and dismissal

(18)
Now, we ask a blessing, as we go to love and serve the Lord ...

May we serve each other by being thoughtful;
May we serve the truth with our integrity;
May we serve the Lord with all our hearts.

pause, followed by blessing and dismissal

(19)

We conclude with a thought to send us on our way...

Lord, turn our prayer into action,
fill our action with your Spirit,
and make our lives a prayer.

pause, followed by blessing and dismissal

(20)

We go now, to find God in our lives ...

We go to find you in familiar faces.
We go to find you in neighbour and stranger.
We go to find you in the poor and suffering.

pause, followed by blessing and dismissal

(21)

Now, we have a sacred moment of sending ...

As we go our separate ways
a single spirit unites us,
a spirit of wanting to make a difference
and make the world a better place.
Send us, Lord, with your Spirit.

pause, followed by blessing and dismissal

(22)

Now, at the final blessing, we make a promise ...

Among my family, I will share your joy
When I'm with my friends, I will radiate your peace
In the midst of strangers, I will show your love.

pause, followed by blessing and dismissal

(23)

We now go to others with the bread of life ...

> We are grateful, Lord –
> now make us generous.
> We are nourished, Lord –
> now we will nourish in turn
> and we will be bread for each other –
> the bread of encouragement,
> the bread of life.

pause, followed by blessing and dismissal

(24)

We ask God to bless us as we go from here ...

> Lord, send us from here –
> with eyes to see signs of hope,
> with hearts to appreciate other people –
> with eyes to see good deeds,
> with hearts to appreciate good intentions.

pause, followed by blessing and dismissal

(25)

The whole Mass has been leading up to this moment ...

> Not a conclusion, but a beginning
> when I take the Eucharist into my daily life,
> into my world,
> to transform everything I do
> and everything I touch.

pause, followed by blessing and dismissal

(26)

Now a thought, to focus on the challenge of this Mass for us ...

I think quietly of somebody I will pay attention to
and be kind and thoughtful to;
and I pray for that person.

pause, followed by blessing and dismissal

(27)

As we conclude we are really only beginning ...

We have received – now it is time to give.
We have received Eucharist – now it is time to give
Eucharist.
We will complete what has happened here
by putting it into practice.

pause, followed by blessing and dismissal

(28)

Now, a blessing prayer, to send us on our way ...

Let a peace descend upon us here,
the peace that Eucharist brings,
to our hearts, to our relationships.
And let peace radiate from us –
in our words, our gestures, our actions.

pause, followed by blessing and dismissal

(29)

We now ask God to send us from here in hope …

> Go from here
> to wherever life calls you.
> Go and take this Eucharist with you.
> Take its blessing and bestow it;
> take its grace and share it;
> take its love and live it.

pause, followed by blessing and dismissal

(30)

Now, we have a sacred moment of sending …

> Outside the doors that I now exit
> there is somebody
> waiting for the joy I will bring
> in my words, my smile, my hope –
> I wonder who that somebody is?

pause, followed by blessing and dismissal

(31)

Before the blessing, a prayer of sending …

> We have spent special time here
> with God and with one another.
> We go now to make time special
> by making time and taking time,
> by having time and giving time
> so that others feel special.

pause, followed by blessing and dismissal

(32)

Now, a thought as we go ...

> We have found you, Lord, in the breaking of bread.
> As we leave this place we will continue finding you
> in the people we meet;
> in the situations we face;
> in the depths of ourselves.

pause, followed by blessing and dismissal

(33)

Just a thought, as we await God's blessing ...

> Somebody said,
> 'When the service is over, the real service begins.'
> In this Eucharist, God has served us
> and ministered to us.
> Now we go to do likewise,
> to minister to one another.

pause, followed by blessing and dismissal

(34)

We pause as we prepare to depart ...

> Our worship is over;
> our service begins.
> We have prayed;
> let our lives become a prayer.
> We are loved;
> let us become love.

pause, followed by blessing and dismissal

(35)
Now, a thought to send us on our way ...

John Paul II said that, when we go from the Eucharist,
'we cannot keep to ourselves the joy we have experienced'.
May the joy of this Eucharist not stay locked inside us;
may we be a source of joy wherever we go.

pause, followed by blessing and dismissal

(36)
We pause for a thought to send us on our way ...

We have not just received the Body of Christ;
we now are the Body of Christ...
We go to live as the Body of Christ
with a care for one another.

pause, followed by blessing and dismissal

(37)
Before the blessing, 'a thought for the road' ...

We all have an influence on one another
so let us be an influence for good.
Let us build each other up.
Let us add to each other's joy
as Christ has done for us.

pause, followed by blessing and dismissal

(38)

We ask the Lord to send us from here ...

Our Mass concludes
but we know it is not complete.
It is only completed
when we bring it with us –
when we live the Eucharist
and communicate its life.
May this be so, Lord Jesus.

pause, followed by blessing and dismissal

(39)

We have prayed together; now we are sent on our mission ...

Jesus said to the person he healed;
'Return to your home
and declare how much God has done for you.'
We go home with thankful hearts.
We bring this experience with us
to whomsoever we meet.

pause, followed by blessing and dismissal

(40)

We go now with this thought ...

Saint Paul tells us that we are 'the aroma of Christ' –
'the fragrance of Christ'.
Live in such a way
that people detect something more –
an aroma of Christ.

pause, followed by blessing and dismissal

(41)

Now, we have a sacred moment of sending …

In this Eucharist, God has built a bridge to humankind.
We will continue building bridges –
to people we are out of touch with –
to people we can't get on with –
to people we don't think of.

pause, followed by blessing and dismissal

(42)

We go from this Eucharist and bring its blessings with us …

Lord, help me believe that, inadequate as I am,
your grace radiates to others from me.
Help me believe that I am a channel of divine love –
that in my weakness is your strength.

pause, followed by blessing and dismissal

(43)

Now, a blessing prayer, to help us as we go …

How often in the gospels Jesus says, 'Do not be afraid.'
Listen as he says to you, 'Do not be afraid.'
Don't let fear stop you – go in the power of his love.

pause, followed by blessing and dismissal

(44)

Let Saint Teresa's prayer inspire us as we leave …

Christ has no body now but yours;
he looks compassionately– through your eyes;
he goes about doing good – with your feet;
he blesses – with your hands;
Christ has no body now but yours.

pause, followed by blessing and dismissal

(45)

Now, a thought as we prepare to depart ...

The only person I can change is myself.
That I may leave this place a changed person,
bringing a new feeling into my relationships,
I pray to you, O Lord.

pause, followed by blessing and dismissal

(46)

Now, a blessing prayer, to send us on our way ...

Jesus said, 'Those to whom much is given,
from them much is required.'
We rejoice in all that we receive;
let us go to express our gratitude
by living generous lives.

pause, followed by blessing and dismissal

(47)

Now, we ask God to send us from here ...

We return to our homes
to our plans for the day,
to the people in our lives.
We bring with us
the courage that the Eucharist gives,
the hope that it gives,
the calm that it gives.

pause, followed by blessing and dismissal

(48)

Now a thought, to focus on the challenge of this Mass for us ...

> We will go from here
> and see each moment as a grace –
> as an opportunity to work for the good of all,
> to make the world a better place –
> to be ambassadors for Christ.

pause, followed by blessing and dismissal

(49)

We pause for a thought to send us on our way ...

> 'Eucharist' means thanks.
> We have given thanks and now we go
> to live our lives in a spirit of thanks –
> to appreciate the gift of life;
> to appreciate others around us –
> to live with thanks in our hearts.

pause, followed by blessing and dismissal

(50)

The whole Mass has been leading up to this moment, when we go forth from here ...

> Jesus the Lord has made a difference to our lives;
> we go now to make a difference –
> to be the best person we can be.

pause, followed by blessing and dismissal

Prayer of the Faithful
for the Three Year Cycle

Year A Sunday 1 of Advent

Isaiah 2:1-5; Psalm 121; Romans 13:11-14; Matthew 24:37-44

Introduction
We look back, rejoicing at Christ's first coming. We look ahead, in expectation of his final coming. We look around, longing for his coming to us this season. Let us pray.

Prayers
May Advent be a time of getting ready for Christ's coming, a time for leaving the darkness and coming into the light.

We pray for all who live in darkness, desolation or despair. May the light of Christ's coming brighten up their lives.

We pray for peace among the nations. May Christ come into people's hearts, dispelling thoughts of conquest, hatred and revenge.

We pray quietly for a moment, to formulate our own special intentions and commitments for this Advent … *(pause)*

We pray for our dead … May they awake to eternal day in the sight of God.

Conclusion
We offer our prayers in praise and thanks to our God, who comes unbelievably close to us in Jesus Christ his Son, who lives and reigns for ever and ever.

Isaiah 11:1-10; Psalm 71; Romans 15:4-9; Matthew 3:1-12

Introduction
Dear God, as you come close to us this Advent, we come close to you with our prayer, confidently awaiting your grace.

Prayers
May Christ's coming inspire us with a spirit of repentance. May we let go this Advent of whatever is enslaving us.

May Christ's coming fill us with a passion for peace. May God's people do no hurt or harm, but live peaceably together.

We give thanks for all people like John the Baptist, who challenge the hypocrisy and injustice in society.

We pray for people who are struggling. We hope that they won't give up and that they will feel God's supporting hand.

We pray for our dead ... May they praise you, O Lord, and sing to your name.

Conclusion
May your name, O Lord, be blessed for ever and may your praise resound to the ends of the earth. Glory be ...

Isaiah 35:1-6,10; Psalm 145; James 5:7-10; Matthew 11:2-11

Introduction
Today we offer our Advent prayers to God in a spirit of expectation. Come near to us, Lord, as we pray.

Prayers
May God give joy and gladness this Advent. May each of us feel more joy, and help others feel gladness.

We ask God to give new heart to all who are troubled or weary, to all with disabilities, to all who are widowed or orphaned, to all who are bowed down or oppressed.

We pray that Christians everywhere will reach out with joy at Christmas to help others in their need.

We pray for our children. May they experience the wonder of Christmas and may they feel joy at Christ's coming.

We pray for our dead sisters and brothers ... May there be everlasting joy on their faces.

Conclusion
Dear God, as we get nearer to Christmas, we pray that we will get nearer to you, who have come so near to us in Christ your Son, our Lord and Saviour, for ever and ever.

Isaiah 7:10-14; Psalm 23; Romans 1:1-7; Matthew 1:18-24

Introduction
This is the season of Good News, the good news of God's coming among us. In a spirit of anticipation we bring our prayers to the Lord.

Prayers
'Emmanuel – God is with us'; may all people, whatever their situation, feel God's presence in their lives.

God comes to each of us. Like Joseph, may we overcome our fear; may we listen and follow God's voice speaking to us.

We pray for all who are expecting a baby around now. May they feel the joy of Christmas in a special way.

We pray for those who have died … May 'Emmanuel – God is with us' be their joyful refrain forever.

Conclusion
As we offer our prayers, we ask that God our Father and the Lord Jesus Christ send grace and peace to all who are gathered here to pray. Glory be …

Year A Christmas

Vigil: Isaiah 62:1-5; Psalm 88; Acts 13:16-17,22-25; Matthew 1:1-25
Midnight: Isaiah 9:1-7; Psalm 95; Titus 2:11-14; Luke 2:1-14
Dawn: Isaiah 62:11-12; Psalm 96; Titus 3:4-7; Luke 2:15-20
Day: Isaiah 52:7-10; Psalm 97; Hebrews 1:1-6; John 1:1-18

Introduction
With joy in our hearts we celebrate the mystery of the Word made flesh. We rejoice that God has come unbelievably close to us in love. In our happiness we now pray.

Prayers
We pray at Christmas that each one of us will find God, who delights so much in us.

May the Lord bless our families this Christmas with an increase of peace, tranquillity and thoughtfulness.

May the Lord bless our children and make their Christmas happy. We say a special prayer for children who are sick.

We think of people who are alone at Christmas and we pray for a more attentive, compassionate society.

We think of those whose Christmas is tinged with sadness. We think of those who are feeling the loss or absence of a loved one.

We pray for our dead … At Christmas we are especially close to our beloved who have died. Let us be glad that they are ringing out their joy to the Lord.

Conclusion
May all of us find it in our hearts this Christmas to praise God and, in the ups and downs of our lives, to be happy that God delights in us. Glory be …

Ecclesiasticus 3:2-6,12-14; Psalm 127; Colossians 3:12-21; Matthew 2:13-15;19-23

Introduction
Jesus, the son of Mary and Joseph, lives in each of us and each of our families. Through him we pray to God.

Prayers
May we live family life with thanks in our hearts, with kindness in our thoughts, with compassion in our actions.

We ask God to look kindly on fathers and mothers and to strengthen them as caring and responsible parents.

We pray for families that have been dispossessed or forced to flee; for families that live in fear and for families that live in a strange land.

We ask God to bless the families we have come from – parents, brothers and sisters, living and dead.

We pray for all who have died ... May they be blessed for ever as members of God's family.

Conclusion
In these and all our prayers we praise the name of Jesus, who grew up with Mary and Joseph and proclaimed the good news of our salvation. Glory be ...

Year A Mary Mother of God

Numbers 6:22-27; Psalm 66; Galatians 4:4-7; Luke 2:16-21.

Introduction
God's Son was born of a woman so that we might all be born into God. Celebrating Mary as Mother of God, we now pray.

Prayers
We pray that we may all be a little like Mary – may we all be mothers of God, for God needs to be born in each one of us.

We pray for mothers and praise God, for they, like Mary, bring life and hope into the world.

We pray on this World Day of Peace for peace among all people, and for peacemakers to be victorious in the world.

On this New Year's Day, we pause in silence to offer to the Lord our hopes for the year ahead … *(pause)*

We pray for our dead … May they share with Mary in glorifying God for ever.

Conclusion
Dear God, as you blessed Mary so greatly, we ask that you be gracious and bless us too and shed your light upon us and give us your peace. We ask this through Christ our Lord.

Ecclesiasticus 24:1-2,8-12; Psalm 147; Ephesians 1:3-6,15-18; John 1:1-18

Introduction
In Christmas season, as we celebrate the mystery of the Incarnation, we pray to God who has come to dwell in our midst.

Prayers
We thank you God for making your home in each of our hearts. May each one of us know the intimacy of your love.

We rejoice that the Word is being made flesh in our world today, every time there is an increase of peace and love and justice.

May the Word be made flesh in our parish, in a new spirit of community and prayer and hope.

May the Light that comes into the world at Christmas shine through the darkness in people's lives.

We pray for our dead … May they experience all the spiritual blessings of heaven.

Conclusion
We praise you, O God, for your Word made flesh, your dwelling for ever with your people, and we say together, Glory be …

Year A Epiphany

Isaiah 60:1-6; Psalm 71; Ephesians 3:2-3,5-6; Matthew 2:1-12

Introduction
On this feast of the Epiphany, Christ is revealed as the light of the world. May our lives be bathed in that light as we now pray.

Prayers
We pray for each person here. As each of us follows our star, may we find Christ in our lives this coming year.

We give thanks for the Christmas season and for the new sense of God's closeness given to us.

May the world recognise Christ as the light of the nations and may all people be united in God.

The wise men were filled with delight at the sight of the star. May your light, O Lord, fill us also with delight.

We pray for our dead ... Gladden them, O Lord, with the light of your face.

Conclusion
We praise you, O God, for your light come into the world and we say together, Glory be ...

Isaiah 42:1-4,6-7; Psalm 28; Acts 10:34-38; Matthew 3:13-17

Introduction
Celebrating the baptism of Jesus, we rejoice that we too have become beloved sons and daughters of God. In a spirit of joy we pray.

Prayers
May each of us have a strong sense of our dignity in God's eyes. May we feel like beloved sons and daughters of God.

May our baptism inspire us to live like Jesus, to go about doing good and making the world a better place.

We pray for the children baptised in our church in the last year. We pray for their parents and for their godparents.

We thank God for our parish baptism team and for the difference they make to people's experience of the sacrament.

We pray for all who have died ... May they experience in full the new life of baptism.

Conclusion
We praise God, whose glory was revealed to us in the baptism of Jesus and we say together, Glory be ...

Year A Ash Wednesday

Joel 2:12-18; Psalm 50; 2 Corinthians 5:20-6:2; Matthew 6:1-6,16-18

Introduction
The word 'Lent' refers to 'lengthening', Springtime, the days getting longer. May it give us the feeling of things brightening up, a feeling of hope as we pray.

Prayers
Lent is about giving alms. May we find a practical way of expressing our solidarity with the poor.

Lent is about prayer. May we set aside a special quiet time of prayer each day during Lent.

Lent is about fasting. May we practise self-restraint during Lent, in whatever way is most appropriate.

We pray that, for many people, Lent will be a time of reconciliation with God and with others.

Let us pray for each other that our plans and hopes for Lent will bear fruit … *(pause)*

Let us pause quietly, to offer to God the thing that we most want to happen during Lent … *(pause)*

Conclusion
May our prayers lead us to feel God's tender compassion, and help us to believe that we can change for the better. We ask this through Christ our Lord.

Genesis 2:7-9; 3:1-7; Psalm 50; Romans 5:12-19; Matthew 4:1-11

Introduction
Jesus, Son of God, was tempted like us. May we be strong like him, through the power of his Spirit, as we pray our Lenten prayers.

Prayers
May Lent be a time when God's mercy washes away our guilt, making our hearts pure and restoring our joy.

May the angels who looked after Jesus in the desert look after all who follow him into the desert this Lent.

We pray for all who are struggling with temptation and trying to change for the better.

May the lengthening days of Lent be a sign of new life for people who are living in darkness or despair.

We pray for all who have died … May the free gift of Christ's grace bring them to life and make them righteous.

Conclusion
Dear God, your Son was faithful to you in the desert. May the fruits of his struggle fall on us and strengthen us on our Lenten journey. We ask this through Christ our Lord.

Year A Sunday 2 of Lent

Genesis 12:1-4; Psalm 32; 2 Timothy 1:8-10; Matthew 17:1-9

Introduction
We take time now to pray, out of our heartfelt trust in Jesus, God's beloved Son.

Prayers
May each day bring us to a deeper faith in Jesus the Son of God.

We pray for all who are struggling, that grace will light their path and sustain them.

May we be gifted with moments of clarity and insight; may this give us a sense of direction and purpose.

We pray for an experience of transformation for all who find life humdrum or monotonous.

We pray for all who have died … May they rejoice in the wonder of God's glory.

Conclusion
We ask you, God, to listen to our prayers and we ask for the grace to listen to your Son, who is Lord for ever and ever.

Exodus 17:3-7; Psalm 94; Romans 5:1-2, 5-8; John 4:5-42

Introduction
We pause to pray on our journey through Lent, our journey into the desert, where we encounter Jesus, our Messiah and our source of life.

Prayers
May we share the joy of the Samaritan woman, who found the meaning of her life in Jesus.

During Lent, as we come face to face with our own spiritual thirst, may we meet Jesus, the living water.

In a spirit of solidarity, we pray for people in different parts of the world whose lives are threatened by drought.

We pray for people who feel abandoned by God, that their hearts will not become bitter or disillusioned.

We pray for all who have died … May they be at peace, their hopes fulfilled in the vision of God's glory.

Conclusion
We praise you, O God, for the love you have poured into our hearts through the Holy Spirit and we say, Glory be …

Year A Sunday 4 of Lent

1 Samuel 16:1, 6-7, 10-13; Psalm 22; Ephesians 5:8-14; John 9:1-41

Introduction
Through Christ our Lord, God has made us children of the light. We pray for God's light to shine into all that is dark in our world and in our lives.

Prayers
We pray for all who will be baptised this Easter and we ask God to enlighten us about what it means to be baptised.

During Lent, may we recognise our own blindness and allow Jesus to help us to see.

May we learn to see the gifts that exist in our community, and may all come to believe how gifted they are.

We pray for those who are blind or partially sighted; may they teach us all to see with the eyes of our hearts.

We pray for our sisters and brothers who have died … May they dwell in the Lord's own house for ever and ever.

Conclusion
Lord, you are our shepherd. Guide us along the right path. May we not fear the darkness but trust in the goodness and kindness you have shown us in Christ our Lord.

Ezekiel 37:12-14; Psalm 129; Romans 8:8-11; John 11:1-45

Introduction
We are approaching the days of Christ's cross and resurrection and we offer our prayers in a spirit of hope and expectation.

Prayers
May the power of Christ free us from forces that imprison us and release the love in our hearts.

We pray for all who are crying to God from the depths of their hearts, that their lives will be transformed.

May the compassion of Jesus touch all those among us who are caring for somebody who is dying.

We pray for all brothers and sisters; may they always feel a special love and care for one another.

We pray for all who have died … May God raise them from their graves and give life to their mortal bodies.

Conclusion
As we make our prayers, O God, we count on your word and we trust in your promise of new life through Christ our Lord.

Year A Palm Sunday

Matthew 21:1-11 (procession); Isaiah 50:4-7; Psalm 22; Philippians 2:6-11; Matthew 26:14-27:66

Introduction
As the crowds welcome Jesus into Jerusalem, so we welcome him into our hearts as we pray.

Prayers
We thank God for the grace we have experienced during Lent and we pray that we will enter fully into the spirit of Holy Week.

We pray for all who are discouraged by failure or frailty, that the passion of Jesus will give them hope.

May we learn to rely on God at all times, just as Jesus did when he was deserted and left alone.

May Jesus, who experienced rejection, be a comfort to all who feel rejected; may he reassure them of God's undying love.

We pray for those who have died ... May Christ in his passion and death lead them to new life.

Conclusion
We offer you, O God, these and all the prayers of our hearts, with confidence in the love you have shown us through Christ our Lord.

Exodus 12:1-8,11-14; Psalm 115; 1 Corinthians 11:23-26; John 13:1-15

Introduction
On this special night we thank Jesus, who made of his death his final gift to us, and we pray.

Prayers
May this special Last Supper meal give us a new appreciation of how much God loves us.

May the washing of feet teach us how to give, to think of others often in life, and to keep the needs of others in mind.

We thank God for all the ways people wash each other's feet, by thinking of each other and caring for one another.

We thank God for our priests; as they lead us in the Eucharist, may they bring us closer to God.

Thinking of Jesus in the Garden of Gethsemane, we pray for people who are facing death tonight.

Conclusion
We praise and thank you, O God, for the mystery that begins to unfold this evening, the mystery of death transformed into new life, in the dying and rising of your Son, who lives and reigns with you and the Holy Spirit, one God for ever and ever.

Year A Easter

Easter Day. Acts 10:34,37-43; Psalm 117; Colossians 3:1-4 (or 1 Corinthians 5:6-8); John 20:1-9
Easter Vigil. Genesis 1:1-2:2; Psalm 103 (or Psalm 32); Genesis 22:1-18; Psalm 15; Exodus 14:15-15:1; Exodus 15; Isaiah 54:5-14; Psalm 29; Isaiah 55:1-11; Isaiah 12; Baruch 3:9-15,32-4:4; Psalm 18; Ezekiel 36:16-28; Psalm 41; Psalm 50; Romans 6:3-11; Psalm 117; Mark 16:1-7

Introduction
Jesus is risen Alleluia! May the joy of these words resound in our hearts and in our gathering as we pray.

Prayers
We pray for all who are baptised this Easter; may Easter give us all a strong sense of what it means to be baptised.

May the lives of Christians radiate the joy and hope of Easter to the world.

May Easter give us a feeling of forgiveness; may we leave sin and guilt behind and start a new relationship with God.

We pray for our children, who bring us Easter's gift of new life. May God bless them.

We pray for our dead … May Christ the morning star bring them the light of life and open everlasting day.

Conclusion
We praise you, O God, for raising Jesus from the dead, for making us a new creation, for bringing hope to the world. Glory be …

Acts 4:42-47; Psalm 117; 1 Peter 1:3-9; John 20:19-31

Introduction
God our Father, in raising Jesus from the dead, you give us a new birth as your sons and daughters. May this fill us with joy as we pray.

Prayers
May we, who have not seen Jesus, come to love him more and more, with a love that radiates joy to those around us.

We pray for people who find it hard to believe, that the eyes of faith may be opened in them.

We pray for all who have become sceptical or cynical about life; may their hearts learn to rejoice again.

May Easter bring us closer together as a community, praising God and supporting one another.

We pray for those who have died ... May they come into an inheritance that can never fade away.

Conclusion
We know, O Lord, that you listen to our prayers. We ask you to listen to us now and we praise you for the joy you have given us in Christ our Lord.

Year A Sunday 3 of Easter

Acts 2:14,22-33; Psalm 15; 1 Peter 1:17-21; Luke 24:13-35

Introduction
Jesus is risen from the dead and he walks alongside us, sharing our hopes and fears. We open our hearts to him as we pray.

Prayers
We ask the risen Jesus to walk with us on the road of life, to fuel our hope and to renew our enthusiasm.

May we recognise Jesus at Mass in the words of scripture and in the breaking of bread, and be changed by the experience.

We pray for all who are feeling disappointed or downcast, that their eyes would be opened to see Jesus walking with them.

We thank God for all the people who live their faith in ordinary ways – and for how this has helped others to believe.

We pray for those who have died … May their hearts rejoice and their souls be glad; may their bodies rest in safety.

Conclusion
Praised be God our creator, who raised Jesus from the dead, who comes to us as the Holy Spirit, who gives us hope, who promises us life, who loves us with a love that is for ever and ever.

Acts 2:14,36-41; Psalm 22; 1 Peter 2:20-25; John 10:1-10

Introduction
Easter means that Jesus is Lord, that he is the true shepherd of our souls, that he is the way to a fuller life. We rejoice in this as we pray.

Prayers
May we trust in Jesus our shepherd, because his voice is familiar. May we hear his voice in every situation.

May faith in Jesus help people to experience life to the full and to savour its delights.

May each person discover their special calling in life and realise the potential they have for enriching the lives of others.

We pray that all God's people will be safe. May the Good Shepherd take care of all who are afraid or living in fear.

We pray for those who have died ... May they dwell for ever in the Lord's own house; may their cup be overflowing.

Conclusion
We praise the Lord who is our shepherd; who gives us rest and revives our spirit; who lights our path and comforts our fear; whose goodness and kindness will follow us all the days of our life, for ever and ever.

Acts 6:1-7; Psalm 32; 1 Peter 2:4-9; John 14:1-12

Introduction
In this Easter season, we proclaim with joy that Jesus is the Way, the Truth and the Life, and we pray that this good news will touch us and change our lives.

Prayers
May Jesus be the Way, the Truth and the Life for each one of us; may we cling to him with all our hearts.

We pray for all who are lost or searching; may Jesus, who is the Way, be the source of guidance for them.

We pray for all who are confused or questioning; may Jesus, who is the Truth, be the source of enlightenment for them.

We pray for all whose lives are weary or listless; may Jesus, who is the Life, be the source of energy for them.

We pray for those who have died … May our prayers accompany them to the place that Jesus has prepared for them.

Conclusion
As we make these prayers, we commit ourselves to continuing the mission of Jesus, so that many will come to believe in him, who is Lord for ever and ever.

Acts 8:5-8, 14-17; Psalm 65; 1 Peter 3:15-18; John 14:15-21

Introduction
The risen Jesus promises to send us the Spirit, so that he will live in us and be with us always. In this Spirit we now pray.

Prayers
May each of us radiate a sense of hope and may the Spirit help us convey to others the reason for our hope.

We ask for courage to witness to our faith – with our family and our friends; in our community and in our work.

We pray that people will welcome the message of the gospel and experience its healing, life-giving power.

We pray with love for people who have been orphaned and for people who do not know their parents.

We pray for those who have died ... May they hear the words of Jesus, 'You will see me, because I live, and you will live.'

Conclusion
We praise the Divine Trinity, Father, Son and Holy Spirit, who has come to live in us so that we might live in God. Glory be ...

Acts 1:1-11; Psalm 46; Ephesians 1:17-23; Matthew 28:16-20

Introduction
Jesus, risen from the dead, sits at God's right hand. He is Lord of heaven and earth, of life and death. We pour out our hearts to him as we pray.

Prayers
May the Ascension assure us that Jesus is present in the world and that his presence is enduring, reliable and powerful.

We pray for people who feel the absence of God and for all who are hesitant to believe. May Jesus reveal himself to them.

Sitting at God's right hand, Jesus is the head of the body. May we be filled with his fullness and be transformed into his body.

Jesus is Lord; may we live by his plan; may we draw on his power; and through our witness, may others come to know him.

We pray for all who have died ... We pray that they are in God's presence and enjoying God's presence completely.

Conclusion
We thank you Lord for the reassurance this feast brings, that you are truly present, that you reign over the world, that you guide all things, that you will come again and bring all things to completion, you who are Lord for ever and ever.

Acts 1:12-14; Psalm 26; 1 Peter 4:13-16; John 17:1-11

Introduction
Jesus is ascended to the Father, his mission accomplished. We, who are still in the world, ask for his Spirit, to fill us with his joy.

Prayers
May the Spirit help us to be confident about our faith and not ashamed; and to handle any unfavourable reaction we get.

As we join together in prayer each Sunday, may our support for each other sustain us in faith and in Christian living.

May Christ's prayer for us strengthen us in our mission of continuing his work in the world.

As Christ watches over the world, we ask him quietly to watch over those we pray for now … *(pause)*

We pray for those who have died … May they enjoy a gladness even greater than we can imagine.

Conclusion
We know that Jesus prays constantly for us, to continue his work of glorifying the Father, who lives with him and the Spirit, one God for ever and ever.

Year A Pentecost

Acts 2:1-11; Psalm 103; 1 Corinthians 12:3-7, 12-13; John 20:19-23 (Vigil: Genesis 11:1-9 or Exodus 19:3-8, 16-20 or Ezekiel 37:1-14 or Joel 3:1-5; Psalm 103; Romans 8:22-27; John 7:37-39)

Introduction

Today, the gift of Easter is completed; the Spirit that Jesus promised is given to us. We pray for the outpouring of the Spirit on the world, on the church and on ourselves.

Prayers

We pray for the church, born at Pentecost. May the Spirit fill us with courage, to be witnesses of Jesus in the world.

God's Spirit works in people in such different ways. May we appreciate our own gifts and the gifts of each other.

We pray for the boys and girls confirmed this year. May God's Spirit build up their spirit and help their personalities to flower.

We pray that the Spirit will renew the face of the earth, teaching people to cherish one another and not to hurt or exploit.

We pray for all who have died ... Send forth your Spirit, O Lord, and bring them to their inheritance as your cherished children.

Conclusion

We praise and thank you, Lord, for the gift of the Holy Spirit, the total gift of yourself, to be with us in all times and situations, so that we may be in you, now and forever.

Exodus 34:4-6, 8-9; Daniel 3:52-56 (psalm); 2 Corinthians 13:11-13; John 3:16-18

Introduction
In the mystery of the Trinity, God has revealed to us God's own deepest self. We rejoice that we have been graced with this revelation and we pray.

Prayers
May this Holy Trinity – the grace of Jesus, the love of God and the fellowship of the Spirit – make a home in our hearts.

We pray for families – in their relationships, may they experience the grace, love and fellowship of the Trinity.

May many hearts delight in the God we glorify today – the gentle, faithful God of Jesus, ever kind and compassionate.

We pray for our world. May relationships of greed and exploitation give way to relationships of grace and solidarity.

We pray for those who have died … May the Holy Spirit bring them to Christ, to share in his glory as children of God.

Conclusion
We gather these and all our prayers into our great prayer in praise of God, the Blessed Trinity of Love. Glory be …

147

Year A Body and Blood of Christ

Deuteronomy 8:2-3, 14-16; Psalm 147; 1 Corinthians 10:16-17; John 6:51-58

Introduction
In Christ's body broken for us and his blood poured out for us, we receive the gift of God, who is undying Love. With thankful hearts we pray.

Prayers
May the Eucharist give life to all who receive it; may it sustain us on our journey and guide us in the wilderness.

May communion with Christ bind us together as his Body; may we look out for one another and see Christ in each other.

As we receive the bread of life, we pray for those who are hungry in body or in spirit. May Christians be the bread of life for others.

We pray for the children who made their First Communion this year; we ask God to bless them and to bless their families.

We pray for all who have died … May they feast with unending joy at the heavenly banquet.

Conclusion
As we make our prayers, we give thanks for the gift of God to us in the Eucharist; we give thanks for all that this means to us and we say, Glory be …

Deuteronomy 7:6-11; Psalm 102; 1 John 4:7-16; Matthew 11:25-30

Introduction
On this feast of the Sacred Heart, we celebrate the love of God given to us in Jesus and poured into our hearts by the Holy Spirit. And we pray.

Prayers
We pray for all who are lost or wounded or overburdened. May Christ guide them lovingly and give them rest.

We pray for all who lack love in their lives. We pray for an abiding confidence in how lovable we are in God's eyes.

We pray for our families. May the love of Jesus fill our hearts and our relationships.

In all the ways that we relate to each other, may we communicate to one another something of God's loving heart.

We pray for all who have died ... May they know the love of Christ and be filled with the utter fulness of God.

Conclusion
We praise you God, who lovingly made us. We praise you Jesus, who lovingly saved us. We praise you Holy Spirit, who lovingly graces each day of our lives. Glory be ...

Year A Sunday 2 of Ordinary Time

Isaiah 49:3,5-6; Psalm 39; 1 Corinthians 1:1-3; John 1:29-34

Introduction

In our Mass today, we welcome into our hearts the Lamb of God who takes away the sins of the world, and we pray.

Prayers

We ask Jesus to lift from us our burden of sin and guilt and to release the love that is locked up in our hearts.

May more and more people come to know Jesus and experience in their lives the power of his Spirit.

We pray that the Holy Spirit will revitalise the church in its mission of witnessing to Jesus as the light of the world.

We think of people who would like us to pray for them and we ask that God's Spirit would touch them.

We pray for those who have died ... May they join with all the saints in glorifying God for ever.

Conclusion

We praise you, Lord, that you delight in us. As we offer our prayers, may we feel the delight of knowing your love. We ask this through Christ our Lord.

Isaiah 8:29-9:3; Psalm 26; 1 Corinthians 1:10-13, 17; Matthew 4:12-23

Introduction
We believe in Jesus, the Light of the world. We turn to him, our light and our help, as we pray.

Prayers
May Jesus heal our blindness; may he help us to see more clearly and to respond to life around us.

We give thanks for the gift of sight and we pray for whose vision is impaired and those who cannot see.

We pray for those whose lives are plunged into darkness or depression or despair; may the light of Christ be their strength.

May we be like Jesus, by brightening up the lives of those who are suffering from sickness or disease.

We pray for our dead ... May they see the Lord's goodness and savour the Lord's sweetness in the land of the living.

Conclusion
Jesus, Light of the world, shine light on our path, put hope in our hearts, bring fruit to our work. Glory be ...

Zephaniah 2:3; 3:12-13; Psalm 145; 1 Corinthians 1:26-31; Matthew 5:1-12

Introduction
We rejoice that we are blessed by God and we pray to God that the spirit of the beatitudes may grow in our hearts and in our world.

Prayers
May we be blessed with a strong trust in God's care and with single-minded devotion to serving the Lord.

May we be blessed with a gentle disposition, that we may radiate peace and help ease tensions.

May the Lord bless all who mourn from loss or suffering or oppression. May the Lord bless us with the gift of compassion.

May the Lord bless all who work for what is right and all who suffer for the truth. May their example inspire us.

We pray for all God's children who have died ... May they rejoice in all the happiness and blessings of God's kingdom.

Conclusion
As we offer you these prayers, O Lord, we hope that we may become more truly your witnesses in the world. We praise you together as we say, Glory be ...

Isaiah 58:7-10; Psalm 111; 1 Corinthians 2:1-5; Matthew 5:13-16

Introduction
Jesus says to us that we are to be the salt of the earth and the light of the world. We ask now for the strength of his Spirit as we pray.

Prayers
May our Christian community be a light in this corner of the world, helping to make Christ more visible.

We pray for all who find it hard to believe in themselves and in the light that radiates from them.

We thank God for those who work to end poverty and hunger; they are Christ's light in the darkness.

May many people have the experience of seeing the light and coming to praise God.

We pray for all the dead ... May God raise their heads in glory.

Conclusion
We praise you, O God, for the glint of light in every darkness. We praise you for bringing us enlightenment through Christ our Lord.

Ecclesiasticus 15:15-20; Psalm 118; 1 Corinthians 2:6-10; Matthew 5:17-37

Introduction
In our prayers as followers of Jesus, we ask for the power to live up to his vision ever more, day by day.

Prayers
May we learn the ways of non-violence, always thinking of the other person as kindly as we can.

May all men and women look on one another and think of one another with profound respect.

May the words we speak to each other be honest and may others find us reliable and faithful.

We thank God for those who have taught us the values we live by and those who continue to inspire and challenge us.

We pray for all who have died ... May they see what no eye has seen; may they enjoy all that God has prepared for them.

Conclusion
Dear Lord, as we seek with all our hearts to follow your way, we pray that we will experience happiness, now and forever.

Leviticus 19:1-2,17-18; Psalm 102; 1 Corinthians 3:16-23; Matthew 5:38-48

Introduction
God's sun shines on both the good and the bad. We pray that our love may be generous enough to include all God's people.

Prayers
When we are treated badly, may we learn not to retaliate, but instead to conquer evil with good.

May we think kindly of our enemies and those we are estranged from. May we see a halo over their heads and bless them.

We think of places and situations where people are divided by hatred. We pray for the transforming power of non-violent love.

We thank God for peacemakers in our world, who inspire us to trust in the weapons of love.

We pray for all who have died ... May they experience perfect peace and reconciliation in God's presence.

Conclusion
As we offer you our prayers, O God, we hope that our love will become a more faithful reflection of the perfect love you have shown us in Jesus Christ, who is Lord for ever and ever.

Year A Sunday 8 of Ordinary Time

Isaiah 49:14-15; Psalm 61; 1 Corinthians 4:1-5; Matthew 6:24-34

Introduction
Lord, you are our rock, our stronghold, our fortress. We trust in you, our safety and our strength. We pour out our hearts before you as we pray.

Prayers
May we have the confidence to see God in all the ups and downs of our lives and in all the events in our world.

Lord, help us not to be consumed by the anxieties of life; may we stay focused on what really matters.

May we help one another not to be anxious, to trust in the goodness of life and to live in the present.

We thank God for the birds in the sky and the flowers in the field; may all people have respect for God's creation.

We pray for sisters and brothers who have died … May their souls be still and may they rest in God.

Conclusion
We thank you, O God, for cherishing us and always taking care of us. We bless you as we say, Glory be …

Deuteronomy 11:18, 26-28, 32; Psalm 30; Romans 3:21-25, 28; Matthew 7:21-27

Introduction

Our God is a mighty stronghold and a rock of refuge to us. We express our confidence in God's unfailing support as we pray.

Prayers

May our faith be strong and active, may it influence what we do and say, may it help shape the choices we make.

We pray that we will listen to God's Word, that we will feel its effect, and then put it into practice.

We think of all who are struggling in any way. May God be a rock of refuge for them, and help keep their spirits up.

We pray for people who have lost their homes or are homeless. We pray for victims of landslides or earthquakes, flooding or storms.

We pray for those who have died ... Let your face shine on them, O Lord, and take them to your heart.

Conclusion

We ask you, Lord, to take these prayers to your heart. Show yourself to those we have prayed for. Show yourself to us, who rely on your help. We make our prayers through Christ our Lord.

Hosea 6:3-6; Psalm 49; Romans 4:18-25; Matthew 9:9-13

Introduction
Our God is a welcoming God, whose loving embrace is all-inclusive and who calls us to mirror that love. May God hear us now as we pray.

Prayers
We pray that all will feel welcome at this table. May we be a welcoming community, helping people to feel God's own welcome.

We pray that our worship will be matched by our actions. May we not be self-righteous or prejudiced. May we think of others as Jesus did.

We pray for people who are trying to cope with failure or inadequacy or sin. May God embrace them in their humility.

May nothing shake our belief in God. May we always trust in God and draw strength from our faith.

We pray for our dead ... May God's coming to them be as certain as the dawn and as refreshing as spring rains watering the earth.

Conclusion
We make our prayers, praising you, O God, for believing in us, for forgiving our failures, for challenging us to grow. Glory be ...

Exodus 19:2-6; Psalm 99; Romans 5:6-11; Matthew 9:36-10:8

Introduction
We have gathered together as God's people. We have listened to God's word. Now, we confidently await God's grace, as we put our prayers into words.

Prayers
The Lord calls each person by name. May each of us discover with joy the part we have to play in fulfilling his plan.

We thank God for carrying us in all our troubles. May this teach us to trust.

May we live our lives with joy and confidence, knowing that God's love for us has been sealed in Christ.

We pray for those who are harassed or dejected. May the Lord lift the spirits of all who are trying to cope with the pressures of life.

We pray for those who have died … We entrust them to God, who is faithful from age to age and from life to death.

Conclusion
We praise the Lord who listens to our prayers and we say together; Glory be …

Year A Sunday 12 of Ordinary Time

Jeremiah 20:10-13; Psalm 68; Romans 5:12-15; Matthew 10:26-33

Introduction
Lord, your help never fails, your love is kind, you listen to the needy. You want us to share our needs and hopes with you. So we pray together.

Prayers
May we hear Jesus saying to us, 'Do not be afraid.' May we not be afraid to follow where God leads us.

We ask the Lord to breathe his gentle spirit on all who are gripped by fear – fear of another person, fear of letting go, fear of the future, or some other fear.

May each of us rest content, in the shadow of God's care, knowing that every hair on our head has been counted.

We give thanks for all who proclaim the good news. We thank God for those who have inspired our own faith ... *(pause)*

We pray for all who have died ... May they enjoy completely the divine grace that comes to us as an abundant free gift.

Conclusion
God our creator, we pray because we love you – you who loved us first in Jesus Christ your Son, who lives and reigns for ever and ever.

2 Kings 4:8-11, 14-16; Psalm 88; Romans 6:3-4, 8-11; Matthew 10:37-42

Introduction
We have listened to God's Word and now we offer our prayers, inspired by the Word we have heard.

Prayers
May we welcome God's messengers – the prophet, the holy person – who come our way. May they help us to follow Christ.

May each of us make a difference to the world we live in, by our thoughtfulness and our actions, however small they seem.

We pray that God's love will brighten up our lives. May we find joy in every day. May we find strength in God.

We pray for a new appreciation of what it means to be baptised and to be living a new life in Christ.

We pray for our dead … May they live a new life with the risen Christ.

Conclusion
Lord, ever gracious, listen to our prayer. Lord, ever loving, change our hearts. Lord, ever powerful, transform our world. This we pray in the name of Jesus the Lord.

Zechariah 9:9-10; Psalm 144; Romans 8:9, 11-13; Matthew 11:25-30

Introduction
Jesus says, 'Come to me and I will give you rest.' In our prayer we take up his invitation. We share with him our burdens and our hopes.

Prayers
Jesus was humble of heart. May we be humble too, gentle with one another, sensitive in our words and actions.

We pray for all who labour and are overburdened; all who are bowed down with burdens or with expectations; all who are made to carry a heavy load.

Jesus promises rest for our souls. We ask him to help us to take time to stop, to stand back, to reflect and to pray.

May the desire for peace grow strong in all hearts. May the Spirit of fellowship bring people together.

We pray for our dead … May God who raised Jesus from the dead breathe resurrection life into them.

Conclusion
We will bless your name forever, O God. We thank you for your blessings and we praise you together as we say, Glory be …

Isaiah 55:10-11; Psalm 64; Romans 8:18-23; Matthew 13:1-23

Introduction
Jesus is God's gift to us. Like water from the heavens he satisfies our thirst. Like a seed sown in the ground he gives us new life. Through him we pray.

Prayers
May God's Word speak to our hearts. May it throw light on our questions and make sense of our lives.

May seeds of light and hope grow in our hearts. Amidst the cares of life may we stay in touch with our deeper selves.

We give thanks for all who dedicate themselves to communicating God's Word. May God bless them in their work.

We pray for the conversion of those who destroy the earth. We thank God for all who love the earth and care for it.

We pray for those who have died ... May the seed of divine life come to full flower in God's kingdom.

Conclusion
Loving God, when we hear your Word, may we feel its power. May we know its hope. May we rise to its challenge. May we radiate its joy. We pray through Christ our Lord.

Year A Sunday 16 of Ordinary Time

Wisdom 12:13, 16-19; Psalm 85; Romans 8:26-27; Matthew 13:24-43

Introduction
There is nothing stronger than God's care and providence in our lives. Reassured in this faith we pray.

Prayers
We pray for the conviction that good is stronger than evil. May God strengthen our resolve and help us to strengthen each other.

We are a mixture of good and bad. May our faults teach us to be humble. May we believe in the goodness God sees in us.

May we be able to accept that God accepts us. May we be able to accept others when we find it hard to.

The Spirit helps us when we cannot put our prayers into words. In silence now, we ask the Spirit to bring to God the deepest prayers in our hearts … *(pause)*

We pray for those who have died … May their faults be burned away. May their goodness shine like the sun in God's kingdom.

Conclusion
As we offer our prayers today, we praise your great power, O God, which you have shown to us in Christ our Lord.

1 Kings 3:5, 7-12; Psalm 118; Romans 8:28-30; Matthew 13:44-52

Introduction
We are all searching for the treasure in life. May the Lord accompany us as we search and bless us as we pray.

Prayers
May we find in life the treasure God has put there for us. May nothing stand in the way of finding joy and happiness.

We pray for the wisdom of Solomon. May we set our sights on what is truly worthwhile and be guided by true values.

We pray for all who are searching for meaning and a sense of purpose. We pray for all who despair of finding this treasure.

We pray for the church, that it will be a haven and a home and a revelation to all who are searching.

We pray for all, known and unknown, who have died ... May they come to share God's own glory.

Conclusion
We thank you Lord for the treasure that is life and we praise you for your glory, you who live and reign for ever and ever.

Year A Sunday 18 of Ordinary Time

Isaiah 55:1-3; Psalm 144; Romans 8:35,37-39; Matthew 14:13-21

Introduction

We have come together to be fed with the bread of life. We ask God to feed our own hunger and to feed the hunger of the world.

Prayers

Despite the world's hunger, we know that there is enough for all. May the Lord teach all people the miracle of sharing.

We pray for people who cannot feed themselves – people who are housebound or disabled, and those who care for them.

We pray for priests; may their ministry help us all to be nourished by the bread of life at the Eucharist.

We pray for all who are troubled or worried or threatened. May they trust in the power of Christ's love.

We pray for those who have died ... May there be nothing now between them and the love of Christ.

Conclusion

We bless you God, for you open wide your hand, to feed us when we look to you. Feed us now as we pray to you through Jesus, your Son and our Lord.

1 Kings 19:9, 11-13; Psalm 84; Romans 9:1-5; Matthew 14:22-33

Introduction
Jesus our Lord came across the water to his disciples. He comes to us in our need and in our struggles. We speak to him now.

Prayers
We praise Jesus who watches over us when life is hard. May our trust in him grow stronger and give us confidence.

We pray for the leaders in our church. May the Lord sustain their faith and give them courage.

We pray for all who are struggling with storms and tribulations in life. May we support one another and overcome all fear.

God's voice speaks of peace. We pray that justice and peace will come wherever people are torn apart by fear and hatred.

We pray for those who have died ... After the storms and struggles of life, may they experience the calm of God's peace.

Conclusion
We pray to you, O Lord, because we trust you. We trust in your power and presence in our lives. And we praise your name, you who live for ever and ever.

Year A Sunday 20 of Ordinary Time

Isaiah 56:1, 6-7; Psalm 66; Romans 11:13-15, 29-32; Matthew 15:21-28

Introduction
Jesus said to the woman, 'You have great faith.' We now come to Jesus with the faith that is in our hearts, and we pray.

Prayers
We give thanks for the faith and belief that people have. May we all believe in ourselves, in one another, in life, and in God.

We pray for people of different faiths who live in our country. May this diversity of beliefs be an enrichment to all.

In the spirit of today's gospel, we pray for parents caring for a son or daughter who is ill. We pray for healing.

In our relationships with one another, may each of us have a care for justice. May we act with integrity.

We pray for all who have died … May the faith they had in life find its fulfilment in God's presence.

Conclusion
May all peoples praise you, O God. May the ends of the earth adore you. May all people come to know you, O God. We make our prayers through Christ our Lord. Amen

Isaiah 22:19-23; Psalm 137; Romans 11:33-36; Matthew 16:13-20

Introduction
We follow Jesus because he has a central place in our hearts. We are close to him and now we share with him our prayers.

Prayers
We ask for a deep, personal relationship with Jesus, to know his power and to know his message. We ask this for ourselves and for each other.

Jesus promises to be faithful to his church. We ask him to re-invigorate the church with the energy of his Spirit.

We pray for leaders in our church. We pray for leadership that is humble and inspiring, blessed with vision and integrity.

Thinking of people in authority, we pray for parents. May they act wisely and be confident of God's presence and support.

We pray for all who have died ... May they adore and glorify God forever.

Conclusion
How rich are your depths, O Lord! How wonderful your wisdom! To you be praise and glory for ever and ever.

Year A Sunday 22 of Ordinary Time

Jeremiah 20:7-9; Psalm 62; Romans 12:1-2; Matthew 16:21-27

Introduction
God is always waiting to listen to our prayers and to fill our hearts with hope. With trust and confidence we now pray.

Prayers
We rejoice that people take up their cross and follow Jesus in so many ways. We rejoice in their generosity and self-sacrifice.

May we let go of whatever prevents us from following Jesus. May we model our lives on the gospel, and find the path to true goodness.

In a spirit of solidarity, we pray for people in different parts of the world who suffer for preaching or living the gospel.

So many people are thirsting for God. We pray that people will find God in their lives and will know God's love.

We pray for those who have died ... May they praise God with joy. May they rejoice and be filled at God's banquet.

Conclusion
Your love, O God, is the greatest thing we know. We praise you, with our lips and with our hearts, as we say; Glory be ...

Ezekiel 33:7-9; Psalm 94; Romans 13:8-10; Matthew 18:15-20

Introduction
Jesus tells us, 'Where two or three meet in my name, I shall be there with them.' We are gathered in his name; we know he is present; and so we pray.

Prayers
In our relationships, when somebody does wrong, may we correct each other gently. May we listen when we do wrong ourselves.

We pray for people who feel excluded from the Christian community. May we reach out and be as welcoming as possible.

Love is the basic commandment. May love be the inspiration guiding every single thing we do or say.

'O that today you would listen to his voice.' Let us quietly listen to what God is saying to each of us today … *(pause)*

We pray for those who have died … May they see the face of God and live.

Conclusion
God in heaven, we are at one in our prayer to you. We ask you to grant our prayer through Christ our Lord.

Year A Sunday 24 of Ordinary Time

Ecclesiasticus 27:30-28:7; Psalm 102; Romans 14:7-9; Matthew 18:21-35

Introduction
We pray to the God of infinite compassion, to fill our hearts and our world with the Spirit of forgiving love.

Prayers
The Lord treats us with compassion and love. May we treat each other in the same way that God treats us.

We pray with distress at the lack of forgiveness in our world. May hard hearts learn to be merciful.

We ask the Lord for a share of his spirit when we ourselves find it hard to forgive.

We pray for people who are treated harshly, for people who don't experience compassion from their fellow human beings.

We pray for those who have died … May the Lord crown them with love and compassion.

Conclusion
We give thanks to you, O God. With all our being we bless your name. May we never forget the blessings you give us. Glory be …

Isaiah 55:6-9; Psalm 144; Philippians 1:20-24, 27; Matthew 20:1-16

Introduction

O God, you are kind and full of compassion. You are close to all who call on you. We now call on you from our hearts.

Prayers

May we have a place in our hearts for everybody and have a special regard for those who get left behind.

May each of us hear God calling us with the words, 'You go to my vineyard too.' May we not be idle. May we do God's work.

We pray for peace in the workplace. May employers be kind and fair and generous. May employees be committed and whole-hearted.

We thank God for all the work we do. We pray that more people will find meaning and satisfaction in their work.

We pray for all who have died. May they praise God's name for ever.

Conclusion

We bless you Lord, day after day. We praise your name for ever. Glory be …

Year A Sunday 26 of Ordinary Time

Ezekiel 18:25-28; Psalm 24; Philippians 2:1-11; Matthew 21:28-32

Introduction
Our God joins us together in the one Spirit. Let us pray now with a single purpose, with one mind and heart.

Prayers
We pray for all who are trying to change for the better. We ask the Lord to give a new beginning to all who have failed in life.

May we be able to change our mind and admit when we are wrong. May the Lord preserve us from self-righteousness.

We ask the Lord to give us eyes to see grace even in the most unlikely places and in the most unexpected hearts.

May we be like Jesus and think of others. May we make room in our minds to make others prominent in our thoughts.

We remember those who have died … We ask God to raise them high, to joyfully acclaim that Jesus is Lord.

Conclusion
Lord, as we pray, we ask you to show us your path. Teach us to walk in your truth, through Christ our Lord.

Isaiah 5:1-7; Psalm 79; Philippians 4:6-9; Matthew 21:33-43

Introduction
In your love, O Lord, you have gathered us as your people. We praise you for the wonderful gift of your love, as we pray.

Prayers
We give thanks for all who are bringing forth the fruits of the Kingdom in the world today – its justice and compassion, its solidarity and peace.

We pray for the church. May it have a new appreciation of Jesus, and of the kingdom we are called to work for.

May the Lord's presence comfort all worried hearts and minds, and bring a feeling of peace to all who are anxious.

May our thinking be guided by the truth. May our motivations be genuine. May we aspire to do what is right and good.

We pray for those who have died … May they rejoice for ever in the communion of saints.

Conclusion
We pray that your peace, O God, which is so much greater than we can understand, will guard our hearts and our thoughts, through Christ our Lord.

Year A Sunday 28 of Ordinary Time

Isaiah 25:6-10; Psalm 22; Philippians 4:12-14, 19-20; Matthew 22:1-14

Introduction
God created us to experience the wonder of life and the joy of divine love. With grateful hearts we pray.

Prayers
May more and more people feel attracted to share the life and joy that God offers us in Christ.

We pray for all who are suffering loss or bereavement. We ask God to wipe away the tears from every cheek.

We pray for the strength of God. May there be nothing we cannot master. May we be ready for anything anywhere.

We ask the Lord our shepherd to revive all whose spirits are drooping and to comfort all who are struggling.

We pray for all who have died ... In the Lord's own house may they dwell for ever and ever.

Conclusion
We praise you, O God; you guide us on the right path; you bless our lives with goodness and kindness, through Christ our Lord.

Isaiah 45:1, 4-6; Psalm 95; 1 Thessalonians 1:1-5; Matthew 22:15-21

Introduction
God's good news comes to us not only as words; it comes with the power of the Spirit, filling us with conviction. In the power of the Spirit we now pray.

Prayers
We pray that everything in our lives – all that we do, all that we say, all that we think – will be done for the greater glory of God.

May each Christian work for a society that is just and equal, inclusive and respectful of all.

We pray for our civil and political leaders, may God's Spirit bless them with vision, integrity and courage.

May we show our faith in action. May we do everything with love. May our hope sustain us and keep us going.

We pray for those who have died ... May they sing a new song to the Lord, full of worship and praise.

Conclusion
We praise you, O God; you listen to the words of our prayers and you give us your Spirit, to help us live our faith with conviction. Glory be ...

Year A Sunday 30 of Ordinary Time

Exodus 22:20-26; Psalm 17; 1 Thessalonians 1:5-10; Matthew 22:34-40

Introduction
We have heard the good news of God's love and we have experienced the joy of the Holy Spirit. In that spirit of joy we now pray.

Prayers
We are all made in the image of God, and God is love. We pray that we may become more loving day by day.

We pray for all who find it hard to love, that they be freed from whatever is blocking up the love within them.

God gives special attention to those who find life hardest. May we too be attentive to those whose needs are greatest.

We thank God for the love we receive and we pray for those who do not experience love in their lives.

We pray for all who have died ... May they know the fullness of love in God's presence.

Conclusion
Through these prayers, O God, give us confidence in our power to love. May our love proclaim to others the good news of your love. We ask this through Christ our Lord.

Malachi 1:14-2:2, 8-10; Psalm 130; 1 Thessalonians 2:7-9, 13; Matthew 23:1-12

Introduction
As a child rests on its mother's breast, so we rest our souls in God, in silence and peace, as we pray.

Prayers
We pray for the leaders in our church; may they practise what they preach and inspire us by their dedication.

We pray for people who have heavy burdens laid on them. May people find the church to be a place of lightness and joy.

We pray for a feeling of unity among all believers. We all have one God; may this teach us to value humility and fellowship.

We pray that God's message will be a living power among us who believe. May its power transform our lives.

We pray for our dead ... Guard their souls in peace before you O Lord.

Conclusion
God our creator, be our protection. Christ our Saviour, guide and teach us. Spirit of the risen Lord, encourage us in Christian living. Glory be ...

Year A Sunday 32 of Ordinary Time

Wisdom 6:12-16; Psalm 62; 1 Thessalonians 4:13-18; Matthew 25:1-13

Introduction
In our prayer today, we open our hearts to God's Wisdom, who sees those who love her and is found by those who look for her.

Prayers
May we be attentive for God's coming to us, in the people we meet, in the events of our lives, in the thoughts of our minds.

We ask God to bear with us in our foolishness and to stay with us when we are slow to appreciate God's presence.

We pray for all who are searching and thirsting for God. May they find peace as they sense how near God is.

We pray for all who are grieving and coping with a loss in their lives. May God renew their hope and their will to keep going.

We pray for those who have died ... May God give them new life in Jesus.

Conclusion
Gracious God, your love is better than life. As we offer you our prayers, show us your strength and glory; and we will bless your name for ever and ever.

Proverbs 31:10-13, 19-20, 30-31; Psalm 127; 1 Thessalonians 5:1-6;
Matthew 25:14-30

Introduction
Dear God, we have listened to your Word, and in response we
offer you now the prayers of our hearts.

Prayers
We thank God for all the gifts and talents among us – for the
unique gifts with which the Spirit blesses each one of us.

We pray for those who do not know their own gifts and who
have little confidence in themselves.

We pray that we may be a community of encouragement, helping each other to rejoice in all that we have to give.

We thank the Lord for all who serve in different ministries in our
parish, using their gifts for the good of others.

We pray for all who have died … They are children of the light.
May Christ bring them to everlasting day.

Conclusion
May God, who created each one of us, teach us to cherish the
beauty within, to appreciate the gifts of others, and to be thankful for the enrichment that such a variety of gifts brings. Glory
be …

Year A Christ the King

Ezekiel 34:11-12, 15-17; Psalm 22; 1 Corinthians 15:20-26, 28; Matthew 25:31-46

Introduction
Risen from the dead, Christ is our Shepherd and King, leading us to share even now in the new life of God's kingdom. Through him we pray.

Prayers
May our society reflect Christ's own regard for those who lack food or clothing, for those who are suffering, for strangers and for prisoners.

We pray for all the people who build Christ's kingdom, giving so much of themselves to others who are suffering or needy.

May we see Christ's face in the face of others. May we put our faith into action by responding to the human needs around us.

We pray for those around us who are lost or wounded or weak. May our prayer lift them up and give them hope.

We remember our sisters and brothers who have died … In the Lord's own house may they dwell for ever and ever.

Conclusion
Lord, may your kingdom come. As we put into practice on earth the values of your kingdom, may we come to see their fulfilment in heaven. We ask this through Christ our Lord.

Isaiah 63:16-17; 64:1, 3-8; Psalm 79; 1 Corinthians 1:3-9; Mark 13:33-37

Introduction
Advent is always welcome, for Christ is always coming, in the world and in the church. As this Advent begins, we pray with expectation.

Prayers
May we stay alert, for Christ comes to us in unexpected ways. May Advent be a time of grace and new beginnings.

We pray for our world, a world waiting for God. We pray that the light of Christ's coming will break through the darkness.

We thank God for the people through whom Christ comes to us each day – family and friends, teachers and witnesses.

We pray quietly for a moment, to think of what we each will do to ready ourselves for Christ's coming this Christmas … *(pause)*

We pray for our dead … We look forward to Christ's coming in glory, when all will be united in him forever.

Conclusion
We are an Advent people, filled with expectation of God coming among us, to refresh our souls and to renew our world. Come in Lord, come among us, today and forever.

Year B Sunday 2 of Advent

Isaiah 40:1-5, 9-11; Psalm 84; 2 Peter 3:8-14; Mark 1:1-8

Introduction
In Advent, we await the Lord coming with power. As we offer our prayers, we make a space for God in our hearts and in our lives.

Prayers
We thank the Lord for people who are like John the Baptist, preparing the way and helping us to connect with Christ.

We ask the Lord to bring consolation to many, and an end to their period of pain or estrangement.

May the Lord help us prepare the way by clearing a space for him in our hearts. May we live holy and saintly lives.

The Lord is not slow to carry out his promises. We pray for all whose trust and patience is faltering.

We pray for all who have died ... We ask you, Lord, to gather them in your arms and hold them against your breast.

Conclusion
Lord God, as we prepare a way for you in our hearts and in our lives, may we celebrate the feast of Christ with love and thanksgiving. We make our prayer in the name of Jesus the Lord.

Isaiah 61:1-2, 10-11; Luke 1:46-50, 53-54 (psalm); 1 Thessalonians 5:16-24; John 1:6-8, 19-28

Introduction
We now offer our prayers in a spirit of joy, giving thanks to God, who comes close to us at Christmas.

Prayers
As we listen to John the Baptist we pray that Christ, the Light of the world, will brighten many lives this Christmas.

We pray that Christ will be born in the world this Christmas, bringing good news to the poor, binding up hearts that are broken, freeing those who are captive.

We pray that Christ will be born in each of our hearts this Christmas, helping us to rejoice and to be happy.

We reach out in our prayer to think of people for whom Christmas is not a happy time or a time they look forward to.

We pray for our brothers and sisters who have died … May they glorify the Lord for ever.

Conclusion
As we offer our prayers, we ask you, O God, to keep us safe and blameless – spirit, body and soul – for the coming of our Lord Jesus Christ, who lives and reigns with you and the Holy Spirit, world without end.

2 Samuel 7:1-5, 8-12, 14, 16; Psalm 88; Romans 16:25-27; Luke 1:26-38

Introduction
This is the season when God pledges love to us for ever in the coming of Jesus. As we pray, we are one with Mary in opening our hearts to this mystery.

Prayers
Mary said 'Yes' to the angel. May we too say 'Yes' and may Christ be born in us this Christmas.

In the coming of Christ, God is doing something wonderful for humanity. May this season fill God's people with wonder.

We pray for people who need someone to come on their behalf. We think of people who are poor or hungry, people who are sad or dispossessed,

We pray that, in the coming days, each of us will put aside some quiet time to allow the meaning of Christmas to sink in.

We pray for our beloved who have died … May they sing for ever of your love, O Lord.

Conclusion
We rejoice that all who need a saviour have that someone in Christ. Dear God, open the hearts of all your people to make room for him, who is Lord for ever and ever.

Vigil: Isaiah 62:1-5; Psalm 88; Acts 13:16-17,22-25; Matthew 1:1-25
Midnight: Isaiah 9:1-7; Psalm 95; Titus 2:11-14; Luke 2:1-14
Dawn: Isaiah 62:11-12; Psalm 96; Titus 3:4-7; Luke 2:15-20
Day: Isaiah 52:7-10; Psalm 97; Hebrews 1:1-6; John 1:1-18

Introduction
With joy in our hearts we celebrate the mystery of the Word made flesh. We rejoice that God has come unbelievably close to us in love. In our happiness we now pray.

Prayers
Lord, bless our families this Christmas with an increase of peace, tranquillity and thoughtfulness.

Lord, bless our children and make their Christmas happy. We say a special prayer for children who are sick.

We think of those whose Christmas is tinged with sadness. We think of those who are feeling the loss or absence of a loved one.

As we share the joy of Christ's coming, may we give others a sense of God's infinite love for them.

At Christmas we renew our hope for peace in the world. May the light of Christ break through the darkness in people's hearts.

We pray for our dead ... At Christmas we are especially close to our beloved who have died. Let us be glad that they are ringing out their joy to the Lord.

Conclusion
In the ups and downs of our lives, may we find it in our hearts to praise God this Christmas and to be happy that God delights in us. Glory be ...

Year B Holy Family

Genesis 15:1-6; 21:1-3; Psalm 104; Hebrews 11:8, 11-12, 14-19; Luke 2:22-40

Introduction
On this feast of the family of Jesus, Mary and Joseph, we place all our families under their protection as we pray.

Prayers
We pray that Christ's love will be at the heart of family life and that all family members will respect and support each other.

In our prayers we reach out to rejoice with all those who have been blessed recently with a child.

We pray with all parents that everything will turn out well for their children. We pray for parents who are worried and anxious.

We pray for older people; like Simeon and Anna, may they bless God for the salvation Christ has won for us.

We pray for all who have died ... May they be blessed for ever as members of God's family.

Conclusion
In these and all our prayers we praise the name of Jesus, who grew up with Mary and Joseph, and proclaimed the good news of our salvation. Glory be ...

Numbers 6:22-27; Psalm 66; Galatians 4:4-7; Luke 2:16-21

Introduction
God's Son was born of a woman so that we might all be born into God. Celebrating Mary as Mother of God, we now pray.

Prayers
We pray that we may all be a little like Mary – that we may all be mothers of God, for God is always needing to be born.

We pray for mothers, and we praise God – for they, like Mary, bring life and hope into the world.

We pray on this World Day of Peace, for peace among all people, and for peacemakers to be victorious in the world.

On this New Year's Day, we pause in silence to offer to the Lord our hopes for the year ahead … *(pause)*

We pray for our dead … May they share with Mary in glorifying God for ever.

Conclusion
Dear God, as you blessed Mary so greatly, we ask that you be gracious and bless us too and shed your light upon us and give us your peace. We ask this through Christ our Lord.

Ecclesiasticus 24:1-2, 8-12; Psalm 147; Ephesians 1:3-6, 15-18; John 1:1-18

Introduction
In Christmas season, as we celebrate the mystery of the Incarnation, we pray to God who has come to dwell in our midst.

Prayers
As God comes to make a home in each of our hearts, may we know and enjoy the intimacy of God's love.

We pray that the Word will become flesh in our world today, as people live the values of peace and love and justice.

May the Word be made flesh in our parish, in a new spirit of community and prayer and hope.

In our prayers we reach out to all who are lonely or sick or in pain or distress this Christmas.

We pray for our dead ... May they experience all the spiritual blessings of heaven.

Conclusion
We praise you, O God, for your Word made flesh, your dwelling for ever with your people, and we say together, Glory be ...

Isaiah 60:1-6; Psalm 71; Ephesians 3:2-3, 5-6; Matthew 2:1-12

Introduction
On this feast of the Epiphany, Christ is revealed as the light of the world. May our lives be bathed in that light as we now pray.

Prayers
We pray for each person here. As each of us follows our star, may we find Christ in our lives this coming year.

We thank God for the Christmas season. We give thanks for the new sense of God's closeness given to us this Christmas.

In the spirit of the wise men, may we offer to the Lord the treasures of our hearts and our lives.

In the midst of all the threats and dangers in the world, may God protect all who are vulnerable and defenceless.

We pray for our dead … Gladden them, O Lord, with the light of your face.

Conclusion
We praise you, O God, for your light come into the world and we say together, Glory be …

Isaiah 55:1-11; Isaiah 12:2-6 (psalm); 1 John 5:1-9; Mark 1:7-11

Introduction
Jesus' baptism was the beginning of his mission among us. We link ourselves to his mission now as we pray.

Prayers
May we hear God saying to us the words spoken to Jesus at his baptism, 'You are my beloved.' May each of us feel beloved by God.

May each of us continue Jesus' mission – may we do good; may we help others to be free; may we be a source of life and hope.

We pray for all the children who have been baptised into our Christian family in recent times, and for their families.

We ask God to bless our baptism team; may their work communicate our welcome to families who are celebrating a new birth.

We pray for all who have died ... We pray with confidence that God delights in them forever.

Conclusion
We praise you, O God, revealed to us as Trinity in the Baptism of your Son. We say together our Trinity prayer of praise, Glory be ...

Joel 2:12-18; Psalm 50; 2 Corinthians 5:20-6:2; Matthew 6:1-6, 16-18

Introduction
The word 'Lent' refers to 'lengthening', Springtime, the days getting longer. May it give us the feeling of things brightening up, a feeling of hope as we pray.

Prayers
Lent is about giving alms. May we find a practical way of expressing our solidarity with the poor.

Lent is about prayer. May we set aside a special quiet time of prayer each day during Lent.

Lent is about fasting. May we practise self-restraint during Lent, in whatever way is most appropriate.

We pray that, for many people, Lent will be a time of reconciliation with God and with others.

Let us pray for each other that our plans and hopes for Lent will bear fruit ... *(pause)*

Let us pause quietly, to offer to God the thing that we most want to happen during Lent ... *(pause)*

Conclusion
May our prayers lead us to feel God's tender compassion, and help us to believe that we can change for the better. We ask this through Christ our Lord.

Year B Sunday 1 of Lent

Genesis 9:8-15; Psalm 24; 1 Peter 3:18-22; Mark 1:12-15

Introduction
In our prayer today we join ourselves with Jesus in the desert and we ask for his Spirit to be with us on our Lenten journey.

Prayers
We pray for all who want Lent to be a special time of grace and growth. May their hopes come true.

During Lent, may God's angels look after us in our fight against sin and temptation.

May our fasting show us practical ways of contributing to the cause of justice and peace in our world.

We pray for adults preparing for baptism this Easter. May our prayer accompany them; may their journey inspire us.

We pray for our dead … May Christ who has entered heaven lead them to God.

Conclusion
We set out on the journey of Lent in the strength of God's Covenant, God's pledge of love to us, helping us repent and helping us rejoice, through Christ our Lord.

Genesis 22:1-2, 9-13, 15-18; Psalm 115; Romans 8:31-34; Mark 9:2-10

Introduction
As we continue our Lenten journey, we ask God to sustain us in our hopes and intentions, and we pray.

Prayers
May we grow in confidence of God's love for us, and God's awareness of us in every situation.

We thank God for moments when we are enlightened, when life's meaning becomes clearer and we are helped to keep going.

Jesus is God's beloved. During Lent, may we listen to him and learn about him and grow to trust him.

May we see God in the ordinary events of life and find God's grace in every moment.

We pray for sisters and brothers who have died … May they enjoy the vision of the glory of Christ.

Conclusion
Dear God, we bless you for coming close to us and revealing yourself to us in Jesus your Beloved, who lives and reigns with you and the Holy Spirit, for ever and ever.

Exodus 20:1-17; Psalm 18; 1 Corinthians 1:22-25; John 2:13-25

Introduction
During Lent we travel with Jesus on the road to Jerusalem, to his cross and resurrection. We ask God to bless us on our journey as we pray.

Prayers
Jesus is God's temple; may our Lenten journey bring us to a greater faith in his resurrection.

May God's Spirit purify and renew our church, so that it may better reflect God's love in the world.

Each of us is a temple of God's Spirit; through the grace of Lent, may we be cleansed and healed and made whole.

May the spirit of the ten commandments permeate our society – a spirit of faith in God and justice in all relationships.

We pray for our brothers and sisters who have died … May they find in God that which is more desirable than anything else.

Conclusion
We ask you Lord to bless us as we pray. We ask you to revive our souls, to gladden our hearts and to give light to our eyes, through Christ our Lord.

2 Chronicles 36:14-16, 19-23; Psalm 136; Ephesians 2:4-10; John 3:14-21

Introduction
We offer our prayers today in a spirit of joy and rejoicing at the great love God shows to us in Jesus.

Prayers
Each of us is created in Christ to be God's work of art. May we live the good life as God meant us to live it.

God loves us so much; may this make a great impression on all who don't feel that love in their hearts.

We pray for people who have taken wrong paths, or who are stuck in wrongdoing; may they experience God's mercy and be changed for the better.

As God loves us so much, may our own hearts be filled with a generous love for every other person without exception.

We pray for all who have died … May they be raised up with Christ and share a place with God in heaven.

Conclusion
We praise you God, infinitely rich in grace, for the goodness you have shown us in Jesus Christ your Son who lives and reigns with you and the Holy Spirit, for ever and ever.

Jeremiah 31:31-34; Psalm 50; Hebrews 5:7-9; John 12:20-30

Introduction
We have been travelling through Lent with Jesus. Now, as the days of his death and resurrection approach, we pray that he will renew us in our commitments.

Prayers
As Jesus goes to his suffering and death, may he give us courage to die to sin and to embrace new life.

We pray that God's grace will touch us deep within, to cleanse us, to wash away our guilt, and to give us new heart.

May all who are suffering draw strength from Jesus, who faced his death with a troubled soul, in humble prayers and silent tears.

As Lent comes to its climax, may many people feel the power of Jesus' cross and resurrection in their lives.

We pray for those who have died ... May Jesus, risen from the dead, draw them to himself.

Conclusion
We glorify God the Father who created us; we glorify Jesus who saves us; we glorify the Spirit who makes us whole; and we say, Glory be ...

Mark 11:1-10 (or John 12:12-16) (procession)
Isaiah 50:4-7; Psalm 22; Philippians 2:6-11; Mark 14:1-15:47

Introduction
On this day the people welcomed Jesus to Jerusalem. We too welcome him as he makes his journey into our hearts this Holy Week.

Prayers
In this week, may our reliving of the passion and death of Jesus bring us to believe more deeply in him as the Son of God.

As we see Jesus being betrayed and mocked and falsely accused, may we be inspired to follow him more faithfully.

We pray for all who suffer, in little ways or great. By the power of Christ's passion, may they give to others.

We pray for all who feel forsaken, like Jesus on the cross. May they feel Jesus identifying with them in their pain.

We pray for all who have died … May they enjoy completely the new life that comes from the cross.

Conclusion
Lord God, as we offer you our prayers, let us experience your gift of new life this Holy Week. We make our prayer through Christ our Lord.

Exodus 12:1-8, 11-14; Psalm 115; 1 Corinthians 11:23-26; John 13:1-15

Introduction
On this special night, Jesus made his death into his final gift to us. We turn to him and we pray.

Prayers
We thank God for the Eucharist and for all that it means to us, and for all the ways it has nourished us.

May the Eucharist we celebrate in memory of Jesus lead us from death to life, from darkness to light, from misery to hope.

May the washing of feet teach us how to receive, to be gracious in accepting help and in allowing others to serve us.

We thank God for parents and teachers, for our priests, for our parish workers and for all who serve among us.

Thinking of Jesus in the Garden of Gethsemane, we pray for people who are facing death tonight.

Conclusion
We praise and thank you, O God, for the mystery that begins to unfold this evening, the mystery of death transformed into new life, in the dying and rising of your Son, who is Lord for ever and ever.

Easter Day. Acts 10:34,37-43; Psalm 117; Colossians 3:1-4 (or 1 Corinthians 5:6-8); John 20:1-9
Easter Vigil. Genesis 1:1-2:2; Psalm 103 (or Psalm 32); Genesis 22:1-18; Psalm 15; Exodus 14:15-15:1; Exodus 15; Isaiah 54:5-14; Psalm 29; Isaiah 55:1-11; Isaiah 12; Baruch 3:9-15,32-4:4; Psalm 18; Ezekiel 36:16-28; Psalm 41; Psalm 50; Romans 6:3-11; Psalm 117; Mark 16:1-7

Introduction
Jesus is risen Alleluia! May the joy of these words resound in our hearts and in our gathering as we pray.

Prayers
May Easter give all of us a new awareness of being baptised into new life. We pray for all who are baptised this Easter.

May we let go of our fears; may we embrace the new life and freedom that Jesus' resurrection has won for us.

We thank God for all the ways in which people bring life out of death and light out of darkness.

We pray for all who are confused or dispirited, that Easter's grace will rekindle their trust in the light.

We pray for our dead ... May Christ the morning star bring them the light of life and open everlasting day.

Conclusion
We praise you, O God, for raising Jesus from the dead, for making us a new creation, for bringing hope to the world. Glory be ...

Acts 4:32-35; Psalm 117; 1 John 5:1-6; John 20:19-31

Introduction
The risen Christ is among us, with his Easter gifts of peace and joy. With thankful hearts we pray.

Prayers
We ask the risen Lord to open the eyes of our hearts, to see what really matters and to see his presence among us.

We pray for those who struggle to believe that Jesus is the Son of God. We ask God to bless us in our doubts and uncertainties.

May Easter give all Christians a strong sense that they are sent by the risen Jesus, to be his witnesses in the world.

May we as a group of believers be united, heart and soul. May we be sensitive to the needs around us.

We pray for those who have died … May they enjoy the love that has no end.

Conclusion
We praise you God our Father for raising Jesus from the dead and sending the Holy Spirit to lead us into new life. Glory be …

Acts 3:13-15, 17-19; Psalm 4; 1 John 2:1-5; Luke 24:35-48

Introduction
The risen Christ comes among us today, and his presence is as real as when he first appeared to the disciples. May we be filled with joy as we pray.

Prayers
May Easter be a time of new beginnings for us – through the power of the risen Lord, may God's love come to perfection in us.

The risen Lord calls us to be his witnesses – may our lives help others to see his presence among us.

May our Eucharist be a real celebration of hope and community, so that many people will recognise Jesus in the breaking of bread.

We pray for all who are unhappy or struggling, that the risen Christ will brighten up their lives and give them courage.

We pray for all who have died … Lift up the light of your face on them, O Lord.

Conclusion
May God our Father, who raised Jesus from the dead, send his Spirit into our hearts and make us his witnesses in the world. We ask this through Christ our Lord.

Acts 4:8-12; Psalm 117; 1 John 3:1-2; John 10:11-18

Introduction
In this Easter season, God invites us to be more aware of our baptism and our vocation in life – to realise that we are loved and that we are called to love. And so we pray.

Prayers
We pray for all who follow the call to love as married people and as parents. May they find joy in living for those they love.

We pray for all who follow the call to love as single people. May they be a gift to all whom they meet.

We pray for all who follow the call to love as priests and religious. May they help others discover their vocation to love.

We pray for all who follow the call to love as widowed or separated people. May they have courage to go on living and loving.

We pray for all who have died ... May they be like God, seeing God as God really is.

Conclusion
We give thanks for the love that the Father has lavished on us by letting us be called God's children. We give thanks for Jesus Christ, the cornerstone of our faith, the good shepherd who loves us now and always, for ever and ever.

Acts 9:26-31; Psalm 21; 1 John 3:18-24; John 15:1-8

Introduction
Jesus is the vine; we are the branches. In our prayer we come close to him and we pray for his life to flow through us.

Prayers
May we make our home in Jesus. May we listen to his word. May our lives bear fruit in a love that is real and active.

We pray for the church, here and everywhere. May it be rooted in Jesus, bear fruit and live in peace.

We are all interconnected, as branches of the vine. We pray now with love for people we know who are suffering in any way.

Jesus says, 'You may ask what you will and you shall get it.' We pause for a moment to ask him for what we need … *(pause)*

We pray for all who have died … May they live for ever, with joy in their hearts.

Conclusion
You, O God, have promised that we shall receive whatever we ask. We ask you now to grant these prayers, tokens of our love and dedication, which we offer through Christ our Lord.

Acts 10:25-26, 34-35, 44-48; Psalm 97; 1 John 4:7-10; John 15:9-17

Introduction
In Jesus, God's love for us has been revealed and we are bathed in infinite love. May the prayers we now make be expressions of love in return.

Prayers
We praise God for all the love in the world – the love of believers and unbelievers, the love of friends and the love of enemies.

We pray for people who find it hard to love; for people who have been hurt or hardened, and for all in whom love has been blocked up.

May we keep close to Jesus, so that God's life and love will flow through us and radiate out from us.

We pray that we may be a community of love, where each person knows the joy of being loved and feeling lovable.

We pray for all who have died … In heaven may they have the completeness of the love they experienced on earth.

Conclusion
Lord, accept these words as tokens of our love for you and of our commitment to live a life of love, to the glory of your name, you who live and reign for ever and ever.

Acts 1:1-11; Psalm 46; Ephesians 1:17-23 (or Ephesians 4:1-13); Mark 16:15-20

Introduction
Jesus, risen from the dead, sits at God's right hand. He is Lord of heaven and earth, of life and death. We pour out our hearts to him as we pray.

Prayers
May the Ascension help us to look beyond the present and to be enthused by the hope that God's call holds for us.

May the Ascension assure us that Jesus is truly the Son of God. May it reassure all who feel doubt or uncertainty.

Jesus remains truly present to us. May we make his presence felt, and may others be drawn to him.

Jesus sits at the right hand of God, always interceding for us. In the quiet of our hearts, we bring our prayers to him ... *(pause)*

We pray for all who have died ... We pray that they are in God's presence and enjoying God's presence completely.

Conclusion
We thank you Lord for the reassurance this feast brings – that you are truly present, that you reign over the world, that you guide all things, that you will come again and bring all things to completion, you who are Lord for ever and ever.

Acts 1:15-17, 20-26; Psalm 102; 1 John 4:11-16; John 17:11-19

Introduction

Jesus has ascended to the Father, his mission accomplished. We, who are still in the world, ask for his Spirit, to fill us with his joy.

Prayers

May we appreciate each other's gifts; may each feel encouraged to bring their gifts into play for the good of all.

We pray that love will make God visible in the world; may we find God in our love for one another.

May Christ's prayer protect us from evil and keep us faithful to our calling.

As Christ watches over the world, we ask him quietly to watch over those we pray for now ... *(pause)*

We pray for those who have died ... May they come to the complete experience of God's love.

Conclusion

We know that Jesus prays constantly for us, that we may continue his work of glorifying the Father, who lives with him and the Holy Spirit, one God for ever and ever.

*Acts 2:1-11; Psalm 103; Galatians 5:16-25; John 15:26-27; 16:12-15
(Vigil: Genesis 11:1-9 or Exodus 19:3-8,16-20 or Ezekiel 37:1-14 or
Joel 3:1-5; Psalm 103; Romans 8:22-27; John 7:37-39)*

Introduction
Today, the gift of Easter is completed; the Spirit that Jesus promised is given to us. We pray for the outpouring of the Spirit on
the world, on the church and on ourselves.

Prayers
We pray for the church, born at Pentecost. In the power of the
Spirit, may we put our faith into action and help renew the face
of the earth.

May the Spirit lead us to know God better. May the Spirit guide
us as we search for the truth.

We thank God for the many ways that the Spirit inspires people
with love and generosity, making the world a better place.

We pray for the boys and girls confirmed this year. May God's
Spirit boost their spirit and help their personalities to flower.

We pray for all who have died … Send forth your Spirit, O Lord,
and bring them to their inheritance as your cherished children.

Conclusion
We praise and thank you, Lord, for the gift of the Holy Spirit, the
total gift of yourself, to be with us in all times and situations, so
that we may be in you, now and forever.

Deuteronomy 4:32-34, 39-40; Psalm 32; Romans 8:14-17; Matthew 28:16-20

Introduction
In the mystery of the Trinity, God has disclosed to us God's own deepest self. We rejoice that we have been graced with this revelation and we pray.

Prayers
May all have a sense of their dignity and destiny, as beloved children of God, sharing in the life and love of the Trinity.

May each of us feel a call to mission, to play our part in communicating God's love in the world.

We pray for people who are searching for God. May the Holy Spirit lead them to Christ and show them the wonder of who God is.

We pray for our world. May all human beings learn to live as a family, in unity and diversity.

We pray for those who have died ... May the Holy Spirit bring them to Christ, to share in his glory as children of God.

Conclusion
We gather these and all our prayers into our great prayer in praise of God the Blessed Trinity of love. Glory be ...

Exodus 24:3-8; Psalm 115; Hebrews 9:11-15; Mark 14:12-16,22-26

Introduction
In Christ's body broken for us and his blood poured out for us, we receive the gift of God, who is undying Love. With thankful hearts we pray.

Prayers
May the gift of Christ's Body and Blood assure us of God's goodness; may it strengthen us to serve God by the way we live.

May we realise that we are the Body of Christ; may we appreciate the wonder of who we are as members of his Body.

As we receive the bread of life, we pray that we will be generous in sharing our goods with others who are in need.

We pray for the children who made their First Communion this year; we ask God to bless them and to bless their families.

We pray for all who have died … May they feast with unending joy at the heavenly banquet.

Conclusion
As we make our prayers, we give thanks for the gift of God to us in the Eucharist; we give thanks for all that this means to us and we say, Glory be …

Hosea 11:1, 3-4, 8-9; (Psalm) Isaiah 12:2-6; Ephesians 3:8-12, 14-19; John 19:31-37

Introduction
On this feast of the Sacred Heart, we celebrate the love of God given to us in Jesus and poured into our hearts by the Holy Spirit. And we pray.

Prayers
We pray that more and more people come to appreciate that God is a God of love and not a God of condemnation.

We pray for all who are lost or wounded or overburdened. May Christ guide them lovingly and give them rest.

We pray for our families. May the love of Jesus fill our hearts and our relationships.

In all the ways that we relate to each other, may we communicate to one another something of God's loving heart.

We pray for all who have died ... May they know the love of Christ and be filled with the utter fullness of God.

Conclusion
We praise you God, who lovingly made us. We praise you Jesus, who lovingly saved us. We praise you Holy Spirit, who lovingly graces each day of our lives. Glory be ...

1 Samuel 3:3-10, 19; Psalm 39; 1 Corinthians 6:13-15, 17-20; John 1:35-42

Introduction
God calls us by name. We pray that each of us will discover with joy what God's call for us is.

Prayers
We pray for all who are trying to work out what their call in life is. May Jesus be a light and a help.

Jesus asks, 'What do you want?' May he help us discover the deepest desires of our hearts.

Jesus says, 'Come and see.' May we find time each day to pray and be quiet in his presence.

We pray that people will respect their own bodies and that sexual relationships will always be an expression of love.

We pray for those who have died … May there be a new song in their mouths, praising and delighting in God.

Conclusion
We thank you, loving God, for hearing our prayer and for guiding us on the right way, through Christ our Lord.

Jonah 3:1-5, 10; Psalm 24; 1 Corinthians 7:29-31; Mark 1:14-20

Introduction
As we offer our prayers, we ask you Lord to look kindly on all of us and on all whom you have called to follow you.

Prayers
May the good news that Jesus brings fill each of our hearts with faith and hope and joy.

May the teaching of Jesus be a challenge to us and help us to change for the better.

We pray for all who feel that Jesus is speaking to them – may they have trust to believe in him and courage to follow him.

We pray for all who are married and bringing up families. May they follow Christ by being the best partners and parents they can be.

We pray for all who have died ... May they share in all the joy of God's kingdom.

Conclusion
Teach us, O God, to see you more clearly, to follow you more nearly, to love you more dearly, day by day. We ask this through Christ our Lord.

Deuteronomy 18:15-20; Psalm 94; 1 Corinthians 7:32-35; Mark 1:21-28

Introduction
We now bring our prayers to God, whose power over all creation has been shown to us in the life of Jesus our Saviour.

Prayers
Through the power of Jesus, we pray that we may be free from forces that dominate and oppress us.

We pray for all who feel themselves in the power of evil spirits; may the power of Jesus protect and liberate them.

We pray with gratitude for all who exercise a ministry of healing – in home or hospital, in our parish and in our society.

We pray that each person – married, single, widowed, celibate – may give themselves to God by the way they live their life.

We pray for all who have died ... May the Lord lead them by the hand to the place of perfect peace.

Conclusion
We praise you, God our creator, for Jesus, who saves us and frees us from all evil. To him be glory for ever and ever.

Job 7:1-4, 6-7; Psalm 146; 1 Corinthians 9:16-19, 22-23; Mark 1:29-39

Introduction

In Jesus we see the depth of God's compassion for us. We confidently bring to him our own needs and the needs of our sisters and brothers.

Prayers

We pray that all who are ill or suffering will feel themselves raised up by Jesus and feel joy again in their lives.

May each of us witness to the good news of the gospel through our compassion for others who are in pain.

We pray that those who are suffering will be a gift to others; may they enrich the lives of those around them.

May the time we spend in prayer, like Jesus, enable us to be a blessing to all whom we meet.

We pray for all who have died ... May they know how great is God's healing and saving power.

Conclusion

Blessed be God. Blessed be Jesus, bringer of God's compassion. Blessed be the Spirit, comforter in all our troubles. Glory be ...

Leviticus 13:1-2, 44-46; Psalm 31; 1 Corinthians 10:31-11:1: Mark 1:40-45

Introduction
We stand before the God of Jesus Christ, who reaches out to touch each one with love. We reach out to God, to share our needs and prayers.

Prayers
May all of us know how much God wants to love us and heal us and see us happy. May we never despair of God's love.

We pray for all whose bodies are being attacked by disease. May the compassion of friends help ease their burden.

We pray with compassion for all who live on the margins or feel excluded, from family or church or society.

May all that we do be done for the glory of God. May we never be offensive to anyone. May we always be helpful to others.

We pray for all who have died … May they ring out their joy in the company of all the saints.

Conclusion
Dear God, may your people, who have brought you their needs and hopes, be filled with joy and freely tell the story of your love wherever they go. We ask this through Christ our Lord.

Year B Sunday 7 of Ordinary Time

Isaiah 43:18-19, 21-22, 24-25; Psalm 40; 2 Corinthians 1:18-22; Mark 2:1-12

Introduction

We all share a special dignity because of Christ and we all carry Christ's Spirit in our hearts. This Spirit links us to God as we pray.

Prayers

May the miracle of God's forgiveness make each of us a new creation and give each of us a new beginning.

We pray for people who are paralysed, for people who have lost a limb, for people who are not as mobile as they used to be.

We pray for all the people who support and carry others who are not able to take care of themselves.

May we have eyes to see the new things that God is doing in the church today. May we embrace the opportunities for renewal.

We pray for those who have died. May they be with the Lord, forever singing God's praises.

Conclusion

We praise you God for all that you do for your people, for your faithful and steadfast love, for your promise of new life. Glory be …

Hosea 2:16-17, 21-22; Psalm 102; 2 Corinthians 3:1-6; Mark 2:18-22

Introduction
We now bring our prayers before God our loving Father, whose tender love and faithfulness are ours forever in Jesus his Son.

Prayers
We pray that following Christ will brighten up our lives and lead us into the joy of the gospel.

We pray for all who find religion heartless or oppressive; may they experience the happiness and delight of the good news.

May we appreciate the value of fasting and self-denial in freeing us to live like Christ and to live for one another.

We pray for all who are imprisoned in guilt; may God's compassionate love heal the pain in their hearts.

We pray for our brothers and sisters who have died ... May they rejoice and be happy at God's heavenly banquet.

Conclusion
As we offer our prayers, we praise God for the new life that is ours through Christ our Lord.

Year B Sunday 9 of Ordinary Time

Deuteronomy 5:12-15; Psalm 80; 2 Corinthians 4:6-11; Mark 2:23-3:6

Introduction
We pray to God who lovingly created us, who frees and transforms us, who always listens when we speak.

Prayers
May our Sundays be special times for remembering God – times for celebrating life, freedom and salvation.

May our Sunday celebration draw us into Jesus' dream, and inspire us to be life-giving and caring.

We thank God for the gift of our hands and we pray for all who are deprived in any way of the use of their hands.

We pray that God will give power to all who are in difficulties and to all who see no answer to their problems.

We pray for those who have died ... May their faces be radiant with the light of Christ's glory.

Conclusion
Loving God, accept these prayers and all the prayers of our hearts; accept the prayers we have no words for; and accept our love as we pray to you through Christ our Lord.

Genesis 3:9-15; Psalm 129; 2 Corinthians 4:13-5:1; Mark 3:20-35

Introduction
We pray to you Lord, out of the depths of our hearts and out of the depths of our faith. May your ears be attentive to the voice of our pleading.

Prayers
May we grow as a family of faith, looking out for each other, and working together to continue the mission of Jesus.

May we be true disciples of Jesus, living by his values, witnessing to his truth and trusting in his Spirit.

May God's grace conquer sin in our world. We pray for all who are victims of violence or injustice, of selfishness or deceit.

May we see with the inner eye of our heart; may our inner selves grow strong, and may troubles not weigh us down.

We pray for all who have died … May God, who raised Jesus to life, raise them with Jesus and place them by his side.

Conclusion
God of love, we praise you for your power, at work in Jesus, lifting us up beyond our limitations. May your power be at work in us now as we pray to you in the name of Jesus our Lord.

Year B Sunday 11 of Ordinary Time

Ezekiel 17:22-24; Psalm 91; 2 Corinthians 5:6-10; Mark 4:26-34

Introduction
In our prayers today, we think about how people grow and change and we marvel at how God works in people's lives and in the world around us.

Prayers
We pray for young people growing up; we pray for adults in their learning and growing; we pray that people will continue to flourish as they grow old.

We pray for trust, and for eyes to see how God is at work in our lives, bringing growth even from small beginnings.

In our church community may people find shelter and feel at home, feel refreshed and encouraged to grow.

We pray for people who work on the land, for people who plant and wait for growth to come.

We pray for all who have died … May they flourish for ever, making their home with the Lord.

Conclusion
We praise you, God, for creating us. We praise you, Jesus, for showing us the way. We praise you, Holy Spirit, source of growth and new life. Glory be …

Job 38:1, 8-11; Psalm 106; 2 Corinthians 5:14-17; Mark 4:35-41

Introduction
We bring our prayers to God, knowing that God cares and is with us in all the ups and downs of our lives.

Prayers
We pray for people we know who are going through troubled times, that the Lord will be with them as a calming presence.

We pray for ourselves; may Jesus be with us when things are difficult; may our fears give way to faith.

For all who work on the sea; for fishing folk, for sailors, for lifesaving and rescue personnel; may they be safe from danger.

We pray for the church; for confidence in Christ's presence amidst storms and tribulations; and for courage amidst fears.

We pray for all who have died ... We pray that God will lead them to the haven they desire.

Conclusion
We praise you, God of all creation, for your care and protection, and for the wonders you do among us. Be with us and for us, now and for ever.

Year B Sunday 13 of Ordinary Time

Wisdom 1:13-15; 2:23-24; Psalm 29; 2 Corinthians 8:7, 9, 13-15; Mark 5:21-43

Introduction
We turn to God our creator, who wants life and health for all that lives, and we ask God to listen to our prayers.

Prayers
We pray for children who are sick and for their families who care and worry; may they feel Christ's healing touch.

We pray for people who have been suffering for long years; we pray for courage to approach the Lord in our need.

We pray for people who are dying, for peace and courage in their fear. We pray for those who accompany them.

We thank God for people who bring healing; may God bless us with a healing touch and give us power to raise each other up.

We pray for all who have died … May God, who wants all to live, raise them up.

Conclusion
We bless you, God, for Jesus your Son, who heals our souls, who turns mourning into dancing, who calls us to raise each other up. May his name be blessed now and for ever.

Ezekiel 2:2-5; Psalm 122; 2 Corinthians 12:7-10; Mark 6:1-6

Introduction
Let us pray. We know that Jesus is here with us. We know that his power is certain. And so we pray with hope-filled hearts.

Prayers
We pray for the people who are like prophets, among our own family and acquaintances – people who show us the face of God.

We give thanks for the prophetic figures in our society. May we allow them to point us to the truth and to true values.

We think of people we know who are sick or suffering. May they have a strong feeling of faith in Jesus to help them keep going.

We pray that our weaknesses, whatever they are, will teach us to find our strength in God

We pray for all who have died ... May they be for ever amazed at the vision of God's glory.

Conclusion
As we pray, we lift up our eyes to the Lord, who dwells in the heavens, our source of strength and mercy and new life. Glory be ...

Year B Sunday 15 of Ordinary Time

Amos 7:12-15; Psalm 84; Ephesians 1:3-14; Mark 6:7-13

Introduction

We have heard the message of the truth and the good news of our salvation; and now we turn to God in prayer.

Prayers

As Jesus sent the apostles in pairs, we pray for a spirit of partnership in our parish; may all share their gifts for the good of each other.

We pray for a spirit of welcome and hospitality in our parish, so that all will feel that they belong.

May we all feel called to do God's work, and may we trust in God to work through us for the good of others.

We pray for all in our parish who are trying to reach out to others with a message of friendship and community.

We pray for all who have died ... May God bless them with all the spiritual blessings of heaven.

Conclusion

We praise you Lord, for blessing us with such richness of grace, for the freedom you bestow on us, and for the peace you promise. Glory be ...

Jeremiah 23:1-6; Psalm 22; Ephesians 2:13-18; Mark 6:30-34

Introduction
We open our hearts in prayer to the Lord, who is our shepherd, who takes pity on us, and looks on us with infinite compassion.

Prayers
May Jesus guide us along the right path. May his teaching nourish us and revive our spirit.

We pray for the priests and lay people who lead us in our parish. May God bless them with wise and caring hearts.

We pray that there will be calm in our lives. May we discover the value of silence and prayer.

We pray for people and countries divided by hostility. May Christ's peace break down the barriers and heal the hatred.

We pray for all who have died ... May their spirits overflow with gladness at the banquet of the Lord.

Conclusion
Dear God, as we offer you our prayers, we ask you to fill our hearts with the goodness and kindness you have shown us in Christ our Lord.

Year B Sunday 17 of Ordinary Time

2 Kings 4:42-44; Psalm 144; Ephesians 4:1-6; John 6:1-15

Introduction
Now, in our prayers, we bring everything to God. And if we feel we have little to bring, we bring God that little.

Prayers
May we all feel the miracle of God's presence, and how much God is doing when we seem to have so little.

We pray for parents as they feed their families; for those who bring food to the housebound; for those who feed the hungry.

We ask God to feed the hunger in our hearts, by teaching us the truth and showing us the way to life.

May we live lives worthy of the name 'Christian', by doing all we can to build unity and peace with our fellow human beings.

We pray for all who have died ... May they thank you, O Lord, as they delight in the abundant blessings of heaven.

Conclusion
We bless you, Lord; with your presence and power among us, there is enough; we bless you that the little we have is enough to be a source of new life. Glory be ...

Exodus 16:2-4; Psalm 77; Ephesians 4:17, 20-24; John 6:24-35

Introduction
We now turn in prayer to God our protector, who nourishes us with the bread of life, to renew us in mind and heart.

Prayers
We pray for faith in Jesus, to feed the deepest hungers of our hearts.

May the bread of life help us to put aside our old ways, and to become the new selves that God wants us to be.

We pray for people who are thirsting for something to believe in, and for people who feel that their lives are aimless.

May all who receive the bread of life do God's work and help reduce the hunger in the world.

We pray for all who have died … May God bring them to that holy land where they will never hunger or thirst again.

Conclusion
We ask you, O God, to listen to these prayers which express our hunger for the life you offer us in Christ our Lord.

Year B Sunday 19 of Ordinary Time

1 Kings 19:4-8; Psalm 33; Ephesians 4:30-5:2; John 6:41-51

Introduction
God our Father draws us to Jesus the Bread of Life, and in our prayer we now ask for that bread to sustain us in all our needs.

Prayers
May the Bread of Life teach us how to live life, with friendship and without spite, with kindness and without grudges.

May Jesus the Bread of Life give us strength to keep going when life's journey gets difficult.

We pray for people who are living in fear or distress; may the Lord be their refuge and rescue them.

We thank God for those who feed us the bread of life – in their care, in their wisdom, in their example, in their generosity.

We pray for all who have died ... May they look towards the Lord and be radiant.

Conclusion
We offer these and all our prayers to God our Father, in the hope that we will draw closer to Jesus, who is our Bread of Life, now and forever.

Proverbs 9:1-6; Psalm 33; Ephesians 5:15-20; John 6:51-58

Introduction
It is God's hospitality and generosity that has gathered us around this table; with thankful hearts we pray.

Prayers
May all who eat at the Lord's table be filled with his Spirit and live their lives with wisdom and thoughfulness.

May the Eucharist give us a spirit of thankfulness that percolates always and everywhere into what we do and say.

We pray for all who are hungering for the bread of life, often without realising it; may they draw life from Jesus.

We pray for the Ministers of the Eucharist in our parish, who help us to share in the bread of life.

We pray for all who have died ... May they lack no blessing as they share in the heavenly banquet.

Conclusion
God our Father, we ask you to listen to our prayers, to satisfy our hungry hearts, to refresh our thirsting spirit, and to lead us on the way you have shown us in Christ our Lord.

Year B Sunday 21 of Ordinary Time

Joshua 24:1-2, 15-18; Psalm 33; Ephesians 5:21-32; John 6:60-69

Introduction
Christ Jesus loves us as his own body, and that is what we are. May the prayers we now offer be filled with his Spirit.

Prayers
We pray with thanks to the Lord, our constant companion on the road of life; may our hearts rest in him.

May Christ's love for us be always in our thoughts; may we follow him with enthusiasm.

The Lord is close to the broken-hearted; we pray to him now for all who are broken-hearted in our community and in our world.

May husbands and wives love each other more than they love themselves, and regard each other with great respect.

We pray for all who have died … May the Spirit of the Lord give them eternal life.

Conclusion
We ask you, Lord, to turn your ears to our appeal and to rescue us from our distress, so that we may bless you at all times, you who live and reign for ever and ever.

Deuteronomy 4:1-2, 6-8; Psalm 14; James 1:17-18, 21-22,27; Mark 7:1-8, 14-15, 21-23

Introduction
Our God is near to us whenever we call, nearer than we can imagine. With hope-filled hearts we pray.

Prayers
We pray for integrity of heart; may we speak the truth and act with justice; may we keep our word and do wrong to nobody.

We pray for all whose hearts are confused or divided, and for all who are trying to find their true selves.

We pray for people whose hearts are heavy; we pray for people whose hearts are broken.

For those who have been turned away from religion. May we offer them a faith that is heartfelt and not mere lip service.

We pray for all who have died ... In the presence of God, may everything be good for them, everything perfect.

Conclusion
Lord, you are nearer to us than our own hearts. As we offer our prayers, we ask that you will be the heart of all that we do and think and say, through Christ our Lord.

Year B Sunday 23 of Ordinary Time

Isaiah 35:4-7; Psalm 145; James 2:1-5; Mark 7:31-37

Introduction
Now we lift up our hearts in prayer to God, who is good to all, who listens to our cries and who comes to save us.

Prayers
We pray for people who are deaf or dumb. We pray for those who find it hard to hear and for those who find it hard to speak.

May each of us speak, not only with our lips, but also from our heart. May our words be spoken with love and be full of hope.

May each of us hear in our hearts the good news of the gospel. May nothing block us from hearing its words of hope.

May we have a high regard for everybody we meet and may we hold everybody in equal respect.

We pray for all who have died … May God, who keeps faith for ever, open their eyes and may they sing for joy.

Conclusion
The Lord Jesus made the deaf to hear and the dumb to speak. May he touch our ears to receive his word and our mouths to proclaim his faith, to the praise and glory of God, who lives and reigns for ever and ever.

Isaiah 50:5-9; Psalm 114; James 2:14-18; Mark 8:27-35

Introduction
Now we bring our prayers to God, who always listens when we call or cry out from our hearts.

Prayers
May we see and love the true face of Christ, the humble servant in whom God's own heart is revealed to us.

We pray for people who are suffering – may Christ who suffered be their companion and encouragement.

We pray for people who are searching – may we all find our true selves by following Christ and giving our lives to him.

May we witness to our faith by the lives we lead, and by our love for people who are suffering or needy.

We pray for all who have died … May they walk in the presence of the Lord in the land of the living.

Conclusion
Blessed be God who hears the cry of our appeal, who keeps our eyes from tears and our feet from stumbling. Glory be …

Year B Sunday 25 of Ordinary Time

Wisdom 2:12, 17-20; Psalm 53; James 3:16-4:3; Mark 9:30-37

Introduction
Lord, may the Word that we have listened to sink into our hearts and guide us as we pray.

Prayers
As we follow Jesus to the cross, may we choose peace instead of power, humility instead of status, gentleness instead of force.

May Jesus' teaching inspire us to think of others often in life and to put the needs of others before our own.

We pray that our children will feel loved and wanted. May we have a special care for all who are innocent or vulnerable.

We pray for those who experience disharmony in their relationships, or within themselves. May God's Spirit sustain them.

We pray for all who have died ... Lord, uphold their lives and save them by your name.

Conclusion
We praise you, O God, for you hear our prayers and listen to the words of our mouths, through Christ our Lord.

Numbers 11:25-29; Psalm 18; James 5:1-6; Mark 9:38-43, 45, 47-48

Introduction
We have listened to what God is saying to us today. Now we ask God to listen, as we in response offer our prayers.

Prayers
We thank God for all the ways that the Spirit is at work – in people who bring hope; in people who are a light in the world.

We pray that our actions and our words will always have a positive effect on others, encouraging and life-giving.

May we not do or say things that affect others badly, causing them to lose heart or lose faith or lose hope.

We pray for the conversion of people whose riches have blinded them to others, and deafened their ears to the cry of the poor.

We pray for all who have died ... May the radiance of God's glory bring absolute joy to them.

Conclusion
We praise you, Loving God, for your law is perfect and your rule is to be trusted. We ask you to guide us in your truth, through Christ our Lord.

Year B Sunday 27 of Ordinary Time

Genesis 2:18-24; Psalm 127; Hebrews 2:9-11; Mark 10:2-16

Introduction
We pray now as God's family, sisters and brothers in Christ, asking for the grace to be faithful to each other as God is faithful to us.

Prayers
We ask God to bless our families, to keep us faithful to each other and to increase our feeling of belonging.

We thank God for the love we have found; we pray for people who feel alone, or are looking for somebody to share their life.

We pray for those whose relationship has failed. In disappointment or guilt, betrayal or failure, may God's undying love help them begin again.

We know how much Jesus loved children; may we convey that love to them and may it bring them great happiness.

We pray for all who have died ... May the Lord one day reunite us with those who have died, never to be separated again.

Conclusion
God of love, we thank and praise you for the love we experience in our life on earth – a foretaste of the inexpressible love we are destined to share with you, for ever and ever.

Wisdom 7:7-11; Psalm 89; Hebrews 4:12-13; Mark 10:17-30

Introduction
You call us to follow you, O Lord. In our prayers, we ask for courage to answer your call.

Prayers
We pray for our world, where so many are enslaved by the pursuit of possessions and money.

We pray for wisdom, to find what really matters, and to give our energies to the things that bring true happiness.

We pray for people who are wealthy; may all of us be true to Christ, whatever the circumstances of our lives.

We pray for courage when we find it hard to give what it costs to follow Christ.

We pray for those who have died ... Lord, shine your glory on them and amaze them with your love.

Conclusion
Through the prayers we say, may we give each other strength in following Christ, who is Lord of our lives, now and for ever.

Year B Sunday 29 of Ordinary Time

Isaiah 53:10-11; Psalm 32; Hebrews 4:14-16; Mark 10:35-45

Introduction
Loving God, you are faithful and you look on us with compassion. We pray to you with hope.

Prayers
We pray that Jesus' suffering and death, in service of us, will bring freedom and forgiveness and new life to many.

May we be like Jesus, serving each other, attending to each other's needs and using our gifts for the good of others.

We thank God for parents and for all who serve, giving themselves for others. May God boost their spirits.

Jesus feels our weaknesses with us – we pray that all who are struggling with temptation will feel his mercy and courage.

We pray for all who have died ... May they see the light of God and be content.

Conclusion
In these and in all our prayers, we say, 'May your love be upon us, O Lord, as we place all our hope in you.' Glory be ...

Jeremiah 31:7-9; Psalm 125; Hebrews 5:1-6; Mark 10:46-52

Introduction
We take courage from Bartimaeus in today's gospel – though blind, he could see who Jesus was. With him, we dare to call for Jesus' help, as we pray.

Prayers
We pray for people who are blind or whose vision is impaired. May others be enriched by their gifts and their humanity.

Like Bartimaeus, may we receive new sight and new understanding, and follow Jesus with new enthusiasm.

We ask God to bless those who work with blind people, and who help give them courage for living.

We pray silently as we hear Jesus saying to us what he said to Bartimaeus, 'What do you want me to do for you?' *(pause)*

We pray for all who have died ... May the Lord comfort them and lead them to streams of living water.

Conclusion
We bless you, O God, for your compassion – for feeling our pain and bending down to us in our need – for soothing our tears and restoring our joy – you who live for ever and ever.

Year B Sunday 31 of Ordinary Time

Deuteronomy 6:2-6; Psalm 17; Hebrews 7:23-28; Mark 12:28-34

Introduction
Lord, you are our rock and our refuge. We call on you with confidence, for your strength and your mighty help

Prayers
May we love God with our whole selves – in wonder and gratitude and closeness. May God be the love of our lives.

May we love others as we would like to be loved ourselves – with real respect, appreciating their grace and beauty.

May we love ourselves as God loves us. May God heal the wounds that prevent us from loving and being loved.

May all God's people experience love in their lives. May they discover that love is their vocation and their life's meaning.

We pray for all who have died … May they rejoice and be completely happy in God.

Conclusion
Christ's power to save is utterly certain; he is living for ever to intercede for all who come to God through him. And so, we make these prayers through Christ our Lord.

1 Kings 17:10-16; Psalm 145; Hebrews 9:24-28; Mark 12:38-44

Introduction
Jesus on the cross had so little left to give, but his giving has been our salvation. We ask him to teach us how to give.

Prayers
We pray for people who feel they have little to give; may they come to believe how rich they are.

We have more, not less, when we share and when we give. May we find joy in giving ourselves and giving our time.

We pray for people who are widowed; may they still hear the call to love and continue to enrich others with their love.

We pray for the conversion of people who exploit those who are weak or poor or vulnerable.

We pray for all who have died ... May Christ appear with salvation to those who are waiting for him.

Conclusion
We bless you, loving God; you teach us that we are most truly ourselves when we give – and most like you, the mystery of giving, who gave yourself completely to us in Christ, who is Lord for ever and ever.

Year B Sunday 33 of Ordinary Time

Daniel 12:1-13; Psalm 15; Hebrews 10:11-14, 18; Mark 13:24-32

Introduction
Jesus tells us, 'Heaven and earth will pass away, but my words will not pass away.' Let us be sure of his presence and power as we pray.

Prayers
We pray that, amidst all the crises and catastrophes of the world, people will trust in the Lord's presence and power.

We pray that we will have a positive attitude, and be alert to the signs of hope in our lives and in the world.

We pray for the church – may it communicate a true vision of life and help people to live wisely.

In Jesus, all sins have been forgiven – may we reach out and grasp the new life he is offering us.

We pray for our sisters and brothers who have died … May they shine as bright as stars for all eternity.

Conclusion
We thank you, Lord, for your coming among us. We praise you for your enduring presence. We look forward to your coming in glory – to be Lord for ever and ever.

Daniel 7:13-14; Psalm 92; Revelation 1:5-8; John 18:33-37

Introduction
Jesus' kingdom is not of this world, but it begins in this world –
in his cross and resurrection – in us, continuing his mission. We
pray for the coming of his kingdom.

Prayers
Jesus's kingdom is a place of truth. May we live by the truth.
May people be truthful with one another.

Jesus's kingdom is a place of unity. May the people of this world
come closer together and celebrate their common humanity.

Jesus's kingdom is a place of freedom. May there be freedom
from oppression. May there be freedom in people's hearts.

Jesus's kingdom is a place of peace. In conflict and division, may
his Spirit turn our minds to thoughts of peace.

We pray for all who have died … May they know the incomparable happiness of seeing God.

Conclusion
Lord, may your kingdom come. As we put into practice on earth
the values of your kingdom, may we come to see their fulfilment
in heaven. We ask this through Christ our Lord.

Year C Sunday 1 of Advent

Jeremiah 33:14-16; Psalm 24; 1 Thessalonians 3:12-4:2; Luke 21:25-28, 34-36

Introduction

This is the season of God's coming near to us in Jesus. We offer our prayers today with a feeling of expectation.

Prayers

May we live the coming weeks in a spiritual way, and allow Christ's coming to have a deep effect on us.

May the Lord's coming be a time of grace; may people become more confident and less fearful, more free and less anxious.

In this season of expectation, we pray for people who have little to look forward to – we pray for light in darkness.

We pause in silence, each of us to think of somebody whom we will keep in our heart during Advent ... *(pause)*

We pray for all who have died ... May they enjoy the Lord's friendship and dwell in perfect peace.

Conclusion

Lord, you once came among us, and you will come again, to transform everything; make us aware of the ways in which you are now coming to birth in our midst – you who live and reign for ever and ever.

Baruch 5:1-9; Psalm 125; Philippians 1:3-6, 8-11; Luke 3:1-6

Introduction
John the Baptist calls on us to prepare a way for the Lord and in that spirit we now pray.

Prayers
May the Lord open our eyes to see his coming into our lives this Advent; may he open a pathway into our hearts.

May the Lord bring us a new awareness of the person he wants each of us to be; may he help us grow in goodness.

May the Lord bring a feeling of relief and release to people whose lives are filled with struggle and tears.

May the Lord come with hope into the sorrows of our world; with harmony into the violence of our world; with integrity into the corruption of our world.

We pray for all who have died ... May they reach the perfect goodness which Christ produces in us for the glory of God.

Conclusion
We offer these prayers with hearts full of expectation of the coming of Christ, who is our Lord and Saviour, now and for ever.

Year C Sunday 3 of Advent

Zephaniah 3:14-18; Isaiah 12:2-6 (psalm); Philippians 4:4-7; Luke 3:10-18

Introduction
Saint Paul tells us: if there is anything you need, pray for it. So, let worry give way to trust, as we pray.

Prayers
May Christ's coming help us to change our ways – may we open our hearts to him by changing for the better.

May Christ's coming inspire us to share with others, to be honest and respectful, and not take advantage of other people.

We pray for people who are bowed down – may they feel the Lord coming near and restoring their joy.

We pray for happiness – may people come to know Christ and discover how happy they can be.

We pray for all who have died ... May they shout with joy and rejoice with all their hearts.

Conclusion
Loving God, we ask you to listen to our prayers and to give us your peace which is so much greater than we can understand – guard our hearts and thoughts through Christ our Lord.

Micah 5:1-4; Psalm 79; Hebrews 10:5-10; Luke 1:39-44

Introduction
On the eve of Christ's incarnation, we open our hearts in prayer, that he may be born again in our world.

Prayers
We ask Christ to come with dignity into the lives of people who feel themselves to be the least in society.

Like with Mary and Elizabeth, may Christ's coming bring a new joy into our relationships.

With Mary, we pray for all mothers, and for all who are carrying a child this Christmas.

Christ is our peace. We ask for his peace for people who are experiencing tension or hurt or division.

We pray for all who have died ... May they be blessed, as the promises made to them by the Lord are fulfilled.

Conclusion
We say with Elizabeth: blessed is the fruit of your womb – Jesus Christ our Saviour, who comes to us to be with us, now and for ever.

Year C Christmas

Vigil: Isaiah 62:1-5; Psalm 88; Acts 13:16-17,22-25; Matthew 1:1-25
Midnight: Isaiah 9:1-7; Psalm 95; Titus 2:11-14; Luke 2:1-14
Dawn: Isaiah 62:11-12; Psalm 96; Titus 3:4-7; Luke 2:15-20
Day: Isaiah 52:7-10; Psalm 97; Hebrews 1:1-6; John 1: 1-18

Introduction
With joy in our hearts we celebrate the mystery of the Word made flesh. We rejoice that God has come unbelievably close to us in love. In our happiness we now pray.

Prayers
Lord, bless our families this Christmas with an increase of peace, tranquillity and thoughtfulness.

Lord, bless our children and make their Christmas happy. We say a special prayer for children who are sick.

We think of those whose Christmas is tinged with sadness. We think of those who are feeling the loss or absence of a loved one.

By the grace of Christmas, may we lead good lives. May we give up what keeps us from God.

We think of people who are living in poverty, and we pray for a spirit of solidarity among human beings.

We pray for our dead ... At Christmas we are especially close to our beloved who have died. Let us be glad that they are ringing out their joy to the Lord.

Conclusion
We praise God this Christmas. In the ups and downs of our lives, we delight that God delights in us. Glory be ...

1 Samuel 1:20-22, 24-28; Psalm 83; 1 John 3:1-2, 21-24; Luke 2:41-52

Introduction
Jesus, the son of Mary and Joseph, lives in each of us and in each of our families. Through him we pray to God.

Prayers
We ask for God's Spirit to guide all our families, to lift up their hearts, and to be with them in the ups and downs of family life.

We pray for sons and daughters growing up; may they discover their gifts and find their way in life.

We ask God to give parents strength of mind and heart, especially when they are anxious about their children.

May God bring peace to families coping with an illness or bereavement; and to families where relationships are strained.

We pray for all who have died, including our own family members ... May they be happy for ever, looking on God's face and singing God's praise.

Conclusion
In these and all our prayers we praise the name of Jesus, who grew up with Mary and Joseph and proclaimed the good news of our salvation. Glory be ...

Year C Mary Mother of God

Numbers 6:22-27; Psalm 66; Galatians 4:4-7; Luke 2:16-21

Introduction
God's Son was born of a woman so that we might all be born into God. Celebrating Mary as Mother of God, we now pray.

Prayers
We pray to be a little like Mary – that God may be born in our hearts.

We pray for mothers and we praise God; for they, like Mary, bring life and hope into the world.

We pray on this World Day of Peace, for peace among all people, and for peacemakers to be victorious in the world.

On this New Year's Day, we pause in silence to offer to God our hopes for the year ahead.

We pray for our dead ... May they share with Mary in glorifying God for ever.

Conclusion
Dear God, as you blessed Mary so greatly, we ask that you be gracious and bless us too and shed your light upon us and give us your peace. We ask this through Christ our Lord.

Ecclesiasticus 24:1-2, 8-12; Psalm 147; Ephesians 1:3-6, 15-18; John 1:1-18

Introduction
In Christmas season, as we celebrate the mystery of the Incarnation, we pray to God who has come to dwell in our midst.

Prayers
May God make a home in each of our hearts; may each of us know in our heart the delight of Gods' love.

May the Word become flesh in our world through the lives we live; may God's life be born in us.

May the Word be made flesh in our parish, in a new spirit of community and prayer and hope.

May the eyes of our minds be enlightened, so that we will be able to see the hope that God's call holds for us.

We pray for our dead ... May they experience all the spiritual blessings of heaven.

Conclusion
We praise you, O God, for your Word made flesh, your dwelling for ever with your people, and we say together, Glory be ...

Year C Epiphany

Isaiah 60:1-6; Psalm 71; Ephesians 3:2-3, 5-6; Matthew 2:1-12

Introduction
On this feast of the Epiphany, Christ is revealed as the light of the world. May our lives be bathed in that light as we now pray.

Prayers
We pray for each person here. As each of us follows our star, may we find Christ in our lives this coming year.

We thank God for the Christmas season which culminates today – and for the new sense of God's closeness given to us this Christmas.

We pray for all who are powerful like Herod, and who are threatened by the truth.

May God's Spirit guide us as we search for the truth and the light; may we grow in wisdom.

We pray for our dead ... Gladden them, O Lord, with the light of your face.

Conclusion
We praise you, O God, for your light come into the world and we say together, Glory be ...

Isaiah 40:1-5, 9-11; Psalm 103; Titus 2:11-14; 3:4-7; Luke 3:15-16, 21-22

Introduction
In the baptism of Jesus, God appears among us and reaches out to us in loving-kindness. With joy-filled hearts we pray.

Prayers
On this feast, may we allow the Spirit of Jesus into our lives, to change our hearts, to heal our spirit, to open up paths before us.

On this day, may we find joy in remembering that each of us is baptised, a beloved child of God.

We pray for people who do not feel that they are loved by God or that they themselves are lovable.

We ask God to bless our parish baptism team; may they help families to feel welcome in the Christian community.

We pray for all who have died … May they receive the blessing that comes with the appearing of our Saviour Jesus Christ.

Conclusion
We praise you, O God, revealed to us as Trinity of Love at the Baptism of Jesus. We praise you, Holy Trinity, as we say, Glory be …

Year C Ash Wednesday

Joel 2:12-18; Psalm 50; 2 Corinthians 5:20-6:2; Matthew 6:1-6, 16-18

Introduction
The word 'Lent' refers to 'lengthening', Springtime, the days getting longer. May it give us the feeling of things brightening up, a feeling of hope as we pray.

Prayers
Lent is about giving alms. May we find a practical way of expressing our solidarity with the poor.

Lent is about prayer. May we set aside a special quiet time of prayer each day during Lent.

Lent is about fasting. May we practise self-restraint during Lent, in whatever way is most appropriate.

We pray that, for many people, Lent will be a time of reconciliation with God and with others.

Let us pray for each other that our plans and hopes for Lent will bear fruit … *(pause)*

Let us pause quietly, to offer to God the thing that we most want to happen during Lent … *(pause)*

Conclusion
May our prayers lead us to feel God's tender compassion, and help us to believe that we can change for the better. We ask this through Christ our Lord.

Deuteronomy 26:4-10; Psalm 90; Romans 10:8-13; Luke 4:1-13

Introduction
The Spirit was with Jesus in the desert. We ask God to give us the same Spirit as we begin our journey through Lent. Let us pray.

Prayers
We pray for each other. May God bless each one here today and help them find what they are searching for during Lent.

May Lent make a difference to our relationship with God. May we love God with all our heart and soul and strength.

We pray for people struggling with temptation. May they see temptation for what it is and have strength to resist.

May Lent be a time of liberation for all who feel oppressed or captive or enslaved.

We pray for all who have died ... May God, who has been with them in life and in death, give them glory.

Conclusion
We know, O God, that everyone who calls on you for help will be saved. In this faith we offer you our prayers through Christ our Lord.

Year C Sunday 2 of Lent

Genesis 15:5-12, 17-18; Psalm 26; Philippians 3:17-4:1; Luke 9:28-36

Introduction
The Lord is our light and our help. May the light of his transfiguration shine in our lives, as we pray.

Prayers
May Lent be a time for listening to God; may we receive a new insight into who Jesus is.

We pray for all whose lives are frantic and lacking peace; for all who are afraid to be still; for all who are missing God.

May Lent be a time for rediscovering what really matters, and letting go of the false gods that rule our lives.

We pray for all who are confused or doubting; may Lent bring a new confidence in God's faithful love.

We pray for all who have died ... May the Lord transfigure their bodies into copies of his glorious body.

Conclusion
In these and in all our prayers, we praise you, O God, for the goodness you have shown us through Christ our Lord.

Exodus 3:1-8, 13-15; Psalm 102; 1 Corinthians 10:1-6, 10-12; Luke 13:1-9

Introduction
Our loving God looks on us with compassion and comes in Lent to deliver us and set us free. We pray to God with hope.

Prayers
May we take Lent seriously, as a God-given opportunity to repent, and not take our faith for granted.

The Lord created us to bear fruit – may each person discover their gifts and the difference they can make in the world.

We pray quietly for one another, that our hopes for Lent will be fulfilled … *(pause)*

We pray for people who are suffering – people we know ourselves – people in our community – people in distant places.

We pray for all who have died … May the Lord bring them to the promised land, where they will know only love and joy.

Conclusion
In our prayers we bless the Lord, who forgives us and heals us and frees us, and who crowns us with love and compassion. Glory be …

Year C Sunday 4 of Lent

Joshua 5:9-12; Psalm 33; 2 Corinthians 5:17-21; Luke 15:1-3, 11-32

Introduction
Lord, we pray to you because we believe – we believe that we can begin again; we believe you can make us a new creation. We pray to you, God of new beginnings.

Prayers
May the church be a place of welcome; may it be like the father of the prodigal son, its arms open in welcoming embrace.

We pray for families where somebody has gone away or lost contact, or where parents and children are estranged.

May Lent arouse a feeling of celebration in our hearts – a feeling of being brought back to life; the start of a new existence.

In this time of grace, may many people be reconciled with God and start on a new path, with hope in their hearts.

We pray for all who have died … May they look towards the Lord and be radiant.

Conclusion
Your praise, O God, is always on our lips. You hear our call and rescue us from our distress. May your glory be sung for ever and ever.

Isaiah 43:16-21; Psalm 125; Philippians 3:8-14; John 8:1-11

Introduction
We believe in a God of new beginnings; we pray to our God, to do new things in our lives and in the world.

Prayers
May we believe the new things God is doing in us; may we follow Christ with eagerness and be changed by knowing him.

May we see what is best in others – may we not judge people by their past, but see their future potential.

We pray for all who have suffered from being judged or condemned or excluded; we pray for a tolerant attitude in society.

May the church be a place of welcome, where people are accepted as they are and encouraged to become their best selves.

We pray for all who have died ... May they reach the prize that God calls us to receive in Christ.

Conclusion
We praise you, O God, for the new things you do in our lives; for the road of hope you make in the wilderness of sin; for always inviting us to begin again. Glory be ...

Year C Palm Sunday

Isaiah 50:4-7; Psalm 22; Philippians 2:6-11; Luke 22:14-23:56

Introduction
We open our hearts in prayer to Jesus, who comes to us in this holiest and most special of all weeks.

Prayers
As Jesus on the cross committed his spirit to God, may we make a new commitment of ourselves during this Holy Week.

May Holy Week be a time of grace – may its prayerful spirit bring reconciliation and hope to many human hearts.

May the Spirit of Jesus be upon all who, like him, are experiencing suffering or failure or rejection.

May the passion of Jesus inspire in his followers a new passion for the values he lived by and the dream he died for.

We pray for all who have died … May they be with Jesus this day in Paradise.

Conclusion
Lord, as the crowds welcomed you into Jerusalem, we too praise you as we say, Glory be …

Exodus 12:1-8, 11-14; Psalm 115; 1 Corinthians 11:23-26; John 13:1-15

Introduction
On this special night, Jesus turned his death into a gift of life. We thank him and pray.

Prayers
May we take to heart what Jesus teaches us tonight – that life is about giving and receiving, serving and being served.

May the Eucharist give us all a feeling of belonging; may we use our gifts to serve each other.

We pray for our families; and we pray that our family meals will be times of companionship and happiness.

We ask God to bless all who serve in our parish, and our priests who lead us in our worship.

Thinking of Jesus in the Garden of Gethsemane, we pray for people who are facing death tonight.

Conclusion
We praise you, O God, for the mystery that unfolds this evening – the mystery of death transformed into new life, in the dying and rising of your Son, who is Lord for ever and ever.

Year C Easter

Easter Day: Acts 10:34,37-43; Psalm 117; Colossians 3:1-4 (or 1 Corinthians 5:6-8); John 20:1-9
Easter Vigil: Genesis 1:1-2:2; Psalm 103 (or Psalm 32); Genesis 22:1-18; Psalm 15; Exodus 14:15-15:1; Exodus 15; Isaiah 54:5-14; Psalm 29; Isaiah 55:1-11; Isaiah 12; Baruch 3:9-15,32-4:4; Psalm 18; Ezekiel 36:16-28; Psalm 41; Psalm 50; Romans 6:3-11; Psalm 117; Luke 24:1-12

Introduction
Jesus is risen Alleluia! May the joy of these words resound in our hearts and in our gathering as we pray.

Prayers
May Easter mean for each of us a renewal of our baptism. With all who are baptised this Easter, may we live a new life.

May Easter be a time of new beginnings, when God will roll away the stone and open up new possibilities in our lives.

This Easter, we pray for transformed hearts and attitudes, for transformed lives and relationships, for a transformed world.

We pray for all our parish workers and for all who have been involved in preparing and ministering at the Easter ceremonies.

We pray for our dead ... May Christ the morning star bring them the light of life and open everlasting day.

Conclusion
We praise you, O God, for raising Jesus from the dead, for making us a new creation, for bringing hope to the world. Glory be ...

Acts 5:12-16; Psalm 117; Revelation 1:9-13, 17-19; John 20:19-31

Introduction
The disciples were filled with joy when they saw the Lord. We ask God to give us the same joy as we pray.

Prayers
The risen Lord came to the disciples on a Sunday. May he come to us with the same joy, the same Spirit, and the same mission.

We thank God for so much faith and hope in people. May the good news of Easter strengthen our faith and boost our hope.

We pray for Easter light for all who are grappling with doubts and questions, and uncertainties about their faith.

May Easter be a new beginning in our Christian community. May the Spirit work through us to attract many people to Jesus.

We pray for all who have died ... May the risen Christ bring them to the love that has no end.

Conclusion
As we offer our prayers, O God, we marvel at what you are doing among us in this Easter time. We rejoice and are glad and we bless your name, now and forever.

Year C Sunday 3 of Easter

Acts 5:27-32, 40-41; Psalm 29; Revelation 5:11-14; John 21:1-19

Introduction
We have felt the stirring of Easter hope in our hearts, and now we express our hope in our prayers.

Prayers
Like the apostles, may we know that the risen Lord sees us in our struggles and comes alongside us as our companion.

May we witness to the hope of the resurrection. We pray for people who are waiting for a word of hope.

May our hearts, like Peter's, fill with love for Jesus. May we follow Jesus gladly and support one another.

We pray for people who feel that they are getting nowhere; may the risen Lord sustain their spirit and lead them forward.

We pray for all who have died ... May the Lord raise their souls from the dead and restore them to life.

Conclusion
As we offer our prayers, O Lord, we join with all creation in these Easter words of hope: All praise, honour, glory and power be yours, for ever and ever.

Acts 13:14, 43-52; Psalm 99; Revelation 7:9, 14-17; John 10:27-30

Introduction
In this Easter time, we rejoice in Christ's rising from the dead and we ask for his Spirit to come upon us as we pray.

Prayers
May we realise that we belong to God and that there is nothing that can take God's love from us.

We pray for all who suffer innocently in our world. May the Lord of Easter lead them to springs of living water.

May the Lord of Easter give us joy and courage, to witness to our faith and spread the good news of the gospel.

Jesus our Shepherd, guide each person to find their true vocation in life and to discover how they can be a gift to others.

We pray for all who have died ... May they come before the Lord, singing for joy.

Conclusion
Lord of life and death, may we feel the new life of Easter, by living lives of joy and hope, in the name of Jesus our Lord, who lives for ever and ever.

Year C Sunday 5 of Easter

Acts 14:21-27; Psalm 144; Revelation 21:1-5; John 13:31-35

Introduction
You, O God, make all things new in the resurrection of your Son.
We ask you to give us new heart, as we bring our prayers to you.

Prayers
This Easter, may we love in a new way. May our love be tender
and thoughtful, giving life and hope to others.

This Easter, may we put our faith into action for all the world to
see, in the way we love one another.

This Easter, may all who find it hard to love have a new feeling
of courage and a new sense of how loved they are.

This Easter, as God gives us new heart, may we give new heart
to each other, to live life with hope.

We pray for all who have died … May they enter into God's own
home, where there is no more mourning or sadness.

Conclusion
In all our prayers we praise you, O Lord. May we glorify you by
living lives of love, as we say, Glory be …

Acts 15:1-2, 22-29; Psalm 66; Revelation 21:10-14, 22-23; John 14:23-29

Introduction
The Holy Spirit is God's Easter gift to us, the Spirit of the risen Jesus. We pray for the gift of the Spirit.

Prayers
May the three-personned God – Father, Son and Spirit – come into each of our hearts and dwell within us.

May the Spirit be our heart's teacher, and help us to appreciate Jesus and his message.

We pray for all whose hearts are troubled or afraid; may Jesus' gift of peace uphold them.

We pray for God's Spirit when we have arguments, to help us listen and be constructive, to build trust instead of fear.

We pray for all who have died ... May they come to the holy city, lit by the radiant glory of God, and be enthralled.

Conclusion
We thank you, O God, for coming to us and making your home in us; for the gift of your Spirit and the gift of your peace – you who live and reign for ever and ever.

Year C Ascension

Acts 1:1-11; Psalm 46; Ephesians 1:17-23 (or Hebrews 9:24-28; 10:19-23); Luke 24:46-53

Introduction

Jesus, risen from the dead, sits at God's right hand. He is Lord of heaven and earth, of life and death. We open our hearts to him as we pray.

Prayers

May the Ascension reassure us of God's power at work in the world; may it fill us with joy and with praise of God.

We pray for people who have little or no joy in their lives. May they feel God's presence renewing their spirit.

Where Jesus has gone, we hope to follow; may this hope be an anchor for our souls, making us calm and secure.

As we look forward to Pentecost, we ask Jesus to fill us with the power of his Spirit, to be his witnesses in the world.

We pray for all who have died ... We pray that they are in God's presence and enjoying God's presence completely.

Conclusion

We thank you Lord for the reassurance this feast brings, that you are truly present, that you reign over the world, that you guide all things, that you will come again and bring all things to completion, you who are Lord for ever and ever.

Acts 7:55-60; Psalm 96; Revelation 22:12-14, 16-17, 20; John 17:20-26

Introduction
Jesus is ascended to the Father, his mission accomplished. We, who are still in the world, ask for his Spirit, to fill us with his joy.

Prayers
We pray for unity between all who believe in Christ; through this unity, may the world come to believe.

We pray that all who thirst for the water of life will hear Jesus' invitation and come to him.

May Christ's prayer for us reassure us, and give us courage and conviction in our calling.

As Christ watches over the world, we ask him quietly to watch over those we pray for now ... *(pause)*

We pray for those who have died ... May Jesus, the bright star of morning, bring them to everlasting day.

Conclusion
We know that Jesus prays constantly for us, that we may continue his work of glorifying the Father, who lives with Jesus and the Spirit, one God for ever and ever.

Year C Pentecost

Acts 2:1-11; Psalm 103; Romans 8:8-17; John 14:15-16, 23-26
(Vigil: Genesis 11:1-9 or Exodus 19:3-8,16-20 or Ezekiel 37:1-14 or
Joel 3:1-5; Psalm 103; Romans 8:22-27; John 7:37-39)

Introduction
Today, the gift of Easter is completed; the Spirit that Jesus promised is given to us. We pray for the outpouring of the Spirit on the world and on the church and on ourselves.

Prayers
May God give the gift of the Spirit to the church, born at Pentecost. May the Spirit live in us and radiate out in our lives.

We pray that the Spirit will renew the face of the earth, and inspire all who work to build a better world.

We pray for the boys and girls confirmed this year. May God's Spirit lift their spirits and help their personalities to flower.

May the Spirit be active in people's lives, and may all know what it feels like to be God's children.

We pray for all who have died ... Send forth your Spirit, O Lord, and bring them to their inheritance as your cherished children.

Conclusion
We praise and thank you, Lord, for the gift of the Holy Spirit, the total gift of yourself, to be with us in all times and situations, so that we may be in you, now and forever.

Proverbs 8:22-31; Psalm 8; Romans 5:1-5; John 16:12-15

Introduction
In the mystery of the Trinity, God has revealed to us God's own deepest self. We rejoice that we have been graced with this revelation, and we pray.

Prayers
We pray for the gift of the Holy Spirit, helping us to know Jesus, and to experience the love of God.

When we bless ourselves, may it always remind us of the Trinity that has made a home in our hearts.

We pray for people who are longing for God. May the Holy Spirit come to them, and satisfy their longing.

May all Christians work for a world of peace and unity, modelled on the loving community of Father, Son and Spirit.

We pray for those who have died ... May the Holy Spirit bring them to Christ, to share in his glory as children of God.

Conclusion
We gather these and all our prayers into our great prayer in praise of God the Blessed Trinity of love. Glory be ...

Year C Body and Blood of Christ

Genesis 14:18-20; Psalm 109; 1 Corinthians 11:23-26; Luke 9:11-17

Introduction
In Christ's body broken for us and his blood poured out for us, we receive the gift of God, who is undying Love. With thankful hearts we pray.

Prayers
May the Body of Christ that we receive unite us to him and strengthen the bonds between us as members of his Body.

May all who participate in the Eucharist be nourished in their spirit, and live with hope and compassion.

We pray for the day when all God's people will have enough. May the Eucharist we receive teach us to share and to care.

We pray for the children who made their First Communion this year; we ask God to bless them and to bless their families.

We pray for all who have died … May they feast with unending joy at the heavenly banquet.

Conclusion
As we make our prayers, we give thanks for all that the Eucharist means to us, and we say, Glory be …

Ezekiel 34:11-16; Psalm 22; Romans 5:5-11; Luke 15:3-7

Introduction
On this feast of the Sacred Heart, we celebrate the love of God given to us in Jesus and poured into our hearts by the Holy Spirit. And we pray.

Prayers
We pray that more and more people come to appreciate that God is a God of love and not a God of condemnation.

We pray for all who are lost or wounded or overburdened. May Christ guide them lovingly and give them rest.

We pray for all who lack love in their lives. We pray for an abiding confidence in how lovable we are in God's eyes.

We pray for our families. May the love of Jesus fill our hearts and our relationships.

We pray for all who have died … May they know the love of Christ and be filled with the utter fullness of God.

Conclusion
We praise you God, who lovingly made us. We praise you Jesus, who lovingly saved us. We praise you Holy Spirit, who lovingly graces each day of our lives. Glory be …

Year C Sunday 2 of Ordinary Time

Isaiah 62:1-5; Psalm 95; 1 Corinthians 12:4-11; John 2:1-11

Introduction
Like Mary, we turn to Jesus in faith and ask him to show us his glory and to meet us in our need.

Prayers
We pray that Jesus, who turned water into wine, will bring an abundance of blessings to all who are in need.

We pray for people who are suffering from drought and who have nothing to drink.

May each of us discover our gifts, the special qualities with which the Spirit has blessed our personalities.

We pray for couples who are getting married; may they always delight in one another and may they find God in their love.

We pray for all who have died ... May they see your glory, O Lord, and may they rejoice in you as you rejoice in them.

Conclusion
We praise the Lord who delights in each one of us. We bless the name of the Lord as we pray together, Glory be ...

Nehemiah 8:2-6, 8-10; Psalm 18; 1 Corinthians 12:12-30; Luke 1:1-4; 4:14-21

Introduction
Jesus comes among us with the good news of God's favour. May this good news bring us joy, as we pray.

Prayers
May the Word of God, proclaimed at Mass, speak to our hearts and give meaning to our lives.

We pray that all people, whatever their need or struggle, will experience the gospel as good news, life-giving and liberating.

We ask God to bless all among us who bring hope and healing to others, for they are messengers of good news.

May we, in this Christian community, act as a single unit, and may we appreciate the different part each one of us plays.

We pray for those who have died ... We ask the Lord to gladden their hearts and to give light to their eyes.

Conclusion
May these prayers, the spoken words of our mouths and the thoughts of our hearts, win favour in your sight, O Lord, our rescuer and our rock, now and for ever.

Year C Sunday 4 of Ordinary Time

Jeremiah 1:4-5, 17-19; Psalm 70; 1 Corinthians 12:31-13:13; Luke 4:21-30

Introduction
The Lord is our rock of refuge, inviting us to trust and to hope as we offer our prayers.

Prayers
We ask God for courage to proclaim the gospel by living good lives, by speaking kindly, by acting justly.

May the Lord give us open hearts, that we may hear his voice in the people around us.

We pray for people who find it hard to love and for people who have known little love in their lives.

May we allow love to be the motivation of all we do or say. May love lead us to God.

We pray for those who have died ... May they see the Lord face to face and know the love that has no end.

Conclusion
For the prayers you have answered, we thank you, O God; and for the prayers which we now offer, we ask your loving response – you who care for us now and forever.

Isaiah 6:1-8; Psalm 137; 1 Corinthians 15:1-11; Luke 5:1-11

Introduction
Lord, you stretch out your hand to us. We pray to you now, knowing that your hand will do all things for us.

Prayers
We ask God to work through each of us, however inadequate we feel. May God's strength show itself in our weakness.

We pray for people who feel that their efforts are in vain, and for people who keep on trusting without seeing any results.

May each person feel called by name, and feel that they have a unique part to play in God's plan.

We ask God to bless all who preach and teach the gospel; may they lead others to faith in Christ.

We pray for those who have died ... May they bless the Lord before the angels and sing for ever to God's glory.

Conclusion
In these and all our prayers, we thank you God for your faithfulness and love, which you have pledged to us through Christ our Lord.

Year C Sunday 6 of Ordinary Time

Jeremiah 17:5-8; Psalm 1; 1 Corinthians 15:12, 16-20; Luke 6:17, 20-26

Introduction
We now bring our prayers to God in a spirit of trust and hope.

Prayers
May we place our hope in Jesus – firmly rooted in him, delighting in his love, not tempted by false gods.

We pray for those who have plenty; may they keep their hearts focused on what really matters in life.

We pray for those who are poor or hungry or struggling; may our solidarity tell them that God is on their side.

We pray for a world where those who have give generously, and those who lack have enough.

We pray for those who have died … May their hopes be fulfilled as they share in Christ's rising from the dead.

Conclusion
We ask you, God, to accept these prayers as tokens of our love for you – you who loved us first in sending Jesus your Son, who is Lord for ever and ever.

1 Samuel 26:2, 7-9, 12-13, 22-23; Psalm 102; 1 Corinthians 15:45-49; Luke 6:27-38

Introduction
In Jesus, God shows us a heart full of compassion and calls us to respond to one another in the same spirit. And so we pray.

Prayers
We pray for all who suffer when others are mean or vindictive or judgemental towards them.

We pray that people will be gracious and generous to one another in their need.

May all God's people think kindly of each other, and be able to bless those who treat them badly.

May we remember God's compassion to us and always try to be compassionate to one another.

We pray for those who have died … May their spirits be transformed in the image of the risen Lord.

Conclusion
In these and all our prayers we give thanks to you, O Lord, and we bless your holy name as we say, Glory be …

Year C Sunday 8 of Ordinary Time

Ecclesiasticus 27:4-7; Psalm 91; 1 Corinthians 15:54-58; Luke 6:39-45

Introduction

We have listened to your Word, O Lord, and now we ask you to listen to our prayers, spoken from our hearts with faith and hope.

Prayers

May each of us see our own imperfections, and realise that the only person we can change is ourselves.

We pray that people would not be judgemental, but learn to see what is good and great in others around them.

May our words always be kind, spoken from a loving heart. May our intentions be positive and our motivation be pure.

We pray for all who find it hard to speak kindly, for all who are harsh or deceitful in their speech.

We pray for those who have died … May their dying be swallowed up in victory and may they know that they did not labour in vain.

Conclusion

God our loving Father, you have spoken your Word to us, from a heart filled with love. May your Word sink deep into our hearts, as we offer you these prayers through Christ our Lord.

1 Kings 8:41-43; Psalm 116; Galatians 1:1-2, 6-10; Luke 7:1-10

Introduction
We come before you, Lord, with our faith and with our prayers. We ask you to listen to our prayers because they are filled with our faith.

Prayers
We pray for ourselves when we feel that we are not worthy – may we hear God's Word and know that we are healed.

We think of all who are sick and of those who care for them – we reach out to touch them with our prayers.

We pray for people who do not worship with us or share our faith – we give thanks for the love of God shining through them.

We pray for people who have come from abroad to make their home among us – we welcome them as we welcome Jesus.

We pray for those who have died … May they live in perfect bliss, their beings transformed by God's undying love.

Conclusion
May all peoples praise and acclaim you, O God, for your strong and faithful love. Glory be …

Year C Sunday 10 of Ordinary Time

1 Kings 17:17-24; Psalm 29; Galatians 1:11-19; Luke 7:11-17

Introduction

The Lord listens and has pity; the Lord comes to our help. And so we now bring our prayers to the Lord.

Prayers

May each of us experience the power of Jesus, bringing us new life; may we follow his call and may our lives be transformed.

We pray for parents who have lost a son or daughter; may they feel God's compassion in their unspeakable grief.

We pray for all who have undergone a loss, whatever it may be; may the Lord gently change their mourning into dancing.

May we allow others to soothe us in our pain. May we be bearers of Jesus' compassion to those around us.

We pray for those who have died … May they praise the Lord, who raises our souls from the dead.

Conclusion

As we offer our prayers, we praise you Lord for the compassion you show us in Jesus your Son, who lives with you and the Holy Spirit, one God for ever and ever.

2 Samuel 12:7-10, 13; Psalm 31; Galatians 2:16, 19-21; Luke 7:36-8:3

Introduction
We have gathered together as God's people. We have listened to God's word. Now, we confidently ask God's grace, as we pray.

Prayers
We praise you, Lord, for your message of forgiveness, and the good news that we are reconciled to God.

The person who is forgiven shows great love. May God's forgiveness release the love in our hearts.

Like King David, may we be humble and truthful when we fail. May we allow others to accept us. May we allow God to love us.

We pray for people who are tormented by guilt. We pray for the burden to be lifted and for peace to take its place.

We pray for our brothers and sisters who have died … May they be fully reconciled in God's love.

Conclusion
We praise the Lord who listens to our prayers and we say together, Glory be …

Year C Sunday 12 of Ordinary Time

Zechariah 12:10-11; Psalm 62; Galatians 3:26-29; Luke 9:18-24

Introduction
We now pray together. As we pray, may each of us feel the power of these prayers touching our hearts and lifting our spirits.

Prayers
We pray for faith to believe in Christ. And we pray for courage to take up our cross and follow him.

We believe in a Saviour who suffered greatly. May this faith bring us strength when things are going against us.

We ask the Lord to help us appreciate that we are, all of us, without exception, equal in respect and dignity.

Our souls are thirsting for God. We pray for one another, that each of us will find God and feel our thirst being satisfied.

We pray for those who have died … May their souls be filled as with a banquet. May their mouths praise God with joy.

Conclusion
In these and all our prayers, we never cease to thank and praise you, O Lord, for your presence and goodness in our lives, as we say, Glory be …

1 Kings 19:16, 19-21; Psalm 15; Galatians 5:1, 13-18; Luke 9:51-62

Introduction

We have gathered as a community of prayer. We are joined to one another in a spirit of prayer. In this unity we now pray.

Prayers

We all want to follow Jesus. May we be single-minded and focused, decisive and dedicated, in responding to his call.

We pray for people who are hearing Jesus' call for the first time. May they feel the newness and excitement of following Christ.

May we be free from the lesser thoughts and desires that enslave us. May we freely follow our best thoughts and desires.

Jesus calls us to love and serve one another. May we be less self-centred and more centred on others.

We pray for our dead ... May they have the fullness of life, and happiness in God's presence for ever.

Conclusion

In all our prayers we praise you, God our creator, for the power of your Spirit working so wonderfully among us – the Spirit you have poured into our hearts through Christ our Lord.

Year C Sunday 14 of Ordinary Time

Isaiah 66:10-14; Psalm 65; Galatians 6:14-18; Luke 10:1-12, 17-20

Introduction

Today we pray that the Lord of the harvest would send labourers to the harvest. We pray that all Christians will be inspired with a sense of mission.

Prayers

May all of us know how gifted we are. May all feel that their contribution is wanted.

We thank God for the many ways in which people give their gifts and time to others.

We pray for all who work to bring peace between individuals, between groups, between religions, between nations.

May the Lord send peace, flowing like a river, into our hearts, into our relationships and into our society.

We remember all who have died ... May they be made altogether new in the Lord.

Conclusion

Loving and powerful God, we offer you these prayers, together with our silent prayers and the hungers of our souls. We praise you for all that you do for us through Christ our Lord.

Deuteronomy 30:10-14; Psalm 68 (or Psalm 18); Colossians 1:15-20; Luke 10:25-37

Introduction
Your Word, O God, is near. It is in our mouths and in our hearts. Help us now to speak our words of prayer.

Prayers
We thank God for the 'good Samaritans' among us. We rejoice that so many people have such an instinct to be compassionate.

We pray for the Samaritans organisation. We pray for the anonymous people they serve who are desperate for help and hope.

We know that God listens to the needy. We pray for all who are in poverty or pain; may God's help lift them up.

God's dream is to reconcile all things in Christ. May the desire for peace be stronger than the violence in the world.

We remember those who have died ... May they enjoy perfect peace in the presence of God.

Conclusion
Your Word, O God, is near, in our mouths and in our hearts. May we put your Word into action, for the glory of your name – you who live for ever and ever.

Year C Sunday 16 of Ordinary Time

Genesis 18:1-10; Psalm 14; Colossians 1:24-28; Luke 10:38-42

Introduction
In our prayers today we welcome Jesus into our hearts and lives. We open our hearts to him as we pray.

Prayers
May our community be welcoming and mindful of others, especially those who might not feel at home with us.

May our society be welcoming, and show hospitality to the stranger in our midst.

In the spirit of Mary in today's gospel, we pray for some quiet time with God during our week.

In the spirit of Martha in today's gospel, we pray that we will be active in doing good.

We pray for those who have died ... May our prayer find them enjoying the vision of God's glory.

Conclusion
We welcome you among us, O God of flesh and blood. We know that you welcome our prayers and that you take them to your heart. Glory be ...

Year A Sunday 5 of Easter

Acts 6:1-7; Psalm 32; 1 Peter 2:4-9; John 14:1-12

Introduction
In this Easter season, we proclaim with joy that Jesus is the Way, the Truth and the Life, and we pray that this good news will touch us and change our lives.

Prayers
May Jesus be the Way, the Truth and the Life for each one of us; may we cling to him with all our hearts.

We pray for all who are lost or searching; may Jesus, who is the Way, be the source of guidance for them.

We pray for all who are confused or questioning; may Jesus, who is the Truth, be the source of enlightenment for them.

We pray for all whose lives are weary or listless; may Jesus, who is the Life, be the source of energy for them.

We pray for those who have died … May our prayers accompany them to the place that Jesus has prepared for them.

Conclusion
As we make these prayers, we commit ourselves to continuing the mission of Jesus, so that many will come to believe in him who is Lord for ever and ever.

Genesis 18:20-32; Psalm 137; Colossians 2:12-14; Luke 11:1-13

Introduction
Jesus teaches us how to pray and to trust that God listens to our prayer. So, let us speak to God with confidence.

Prayers
'Lord, teach us to pray.' May each of us make time to get in touch with God and get in touch with ourselves.

'Ask and it will be given to you.' When we ask for what we want, may we trust God to give us what we need.

'Give us each day our daily bread.' May we each play our part, so that all God's people will have the basic necessities of life.

'He has forgiven all our sins.' May all God's people allow themselves to feel the joy of being forgiven.

We pray for our dead … May the Lord bring them to the light of eternal day.

Conclusion
We thank you Lord for always listening to us when we pray. We praise you for your faithfulness and love as we say together, Glory be …

Year C Sunday 18 of Ordinary Time

Ecclesiastes 1:2; 2:21-23; Psalm 89 (or Psalm 94); Colossians 3:1-5, 9-11; Luke 13:13-21

Introduction
We have listened to God's Word and now we pray that the wisdom of God's Word will sink into our hearts and make us wise.

Prayers
Jesus teaches us the secret of what really matters in life. May we listen to his words and learn how to live well.

May we spend our energy on things of lasting value – such as solidarity and truth, integrity and generosity.

We thank God for the good things of life; may we enjoy them without becoming slaves of pleasures and possessions.

May God's grace help us conquer the greed in ourselves and in the world. May God's grace strengthen our instinct to care.

We pray for all who have died ... May they be renewed in the image of their creator. May they be revealed in all their glory.

Conclusion
We ask you Lord to accept our prayers. May the wisdom of your Word sink into our hearts and make us wise. We ask this through Christ our Lord.

Wisdom 18:6-9; Psalm 32; Hebrews 11:1-2, 8-19; Luke 12:32-48

Introduction
Dear God, you have made us glorious by calling us to you. We rejoice in being your children and we pray.

Prayers
Let us always be ready, for God appears unexpectedly. We pray for open minds, for humble hearts and for a generous spirit.

We think of those who wait for somebody's return – for a missing person, or someone gone away, or an estranged friend.

In the spirit of Abraham, we pray for people who manage to keep going in faith, though they cannot see the end.

We think of foreigners who have travelled here in hope. May we offer them an experience of home.

We pray for all who have died ... May they ring out their joy to the Lord.

Conclusion
May your love be upon us O Lord, as we place all our hope in you. Glory be ...

Year C Sunday 20 of Ordinary Time

Jeremiah 38:4-6, 8-10; Psalm 39; Hebrews 12:1-4; Luke 12:49-53

Introduction
We come to you, Lord, in prayer. As we pray, we ask you to strengthen us in following you.

Prayers
We ask for courage and decisiveness in following Jesus; may we be enthusiastic, and not become complacent.

Jesus came to bring fire to the earth. May the Spirit rekindle that fire in our church, for the good of the world.

We thank God for the people who inspire and encourage us in the way of Jesus. We pray for the gift of endurance.

We pray for all who cry out to God in their need. May the Lord put a new song in their mouth.

We pray for those who have died and gone before us ... May they know the joy that Jesus came to share with us.

Conclusion
Our prayers are a pledge of our love, O God. Sustain us in our commitment, through Christ our Lord.

Year C Sunday 21 of Ordinary Time

Isaiah 66:18-21; Psalm 116; Hebrews 12:5-7, 11-13; Luke 13:22-30

Introduction
Strong is God's love for us, faithful for ever. May this love give us strength as we pray.

Prayers
We pray for mutual respect between people of different beliefs. May all religions help people to experience God.

We are all God's sons and daughters. May this encourage us. May it bear fruit in peace and goodness among us.

When people are down, may they not lose heart. When people do well, may they not become smug. May we trust in God always.

We pray for all who are bowed down with suffering; may they continue to live with faith and hope and love.

We pray for our dead ... May they take their place at the feast in God's kingdom.

Conclusion
We praise you God, alive and active in so many ways in our lives. We praise you through Christ our Lord.

Year C Sunday 22 of Ordinary Time

Ecclesiasticus 3:17-20, 28-29; Psalm 67; Hebrews 12:18-19, 22-24; Luke 14:1, 7-14

Introduction
God, our guide and protector, we have listened attentively to your Word. We ask you now to listen kindly to our prayer.

Prayers
We pray for a world where dignity is more important than status, and where giving is valued more than getting.

We pray for those with a special place in God's heart – the orphaned, the widowed, the lonely, the homeless, the prisoner, the starving, the poor, the disabled.

May everyone feel recognised and appreciated; may each of us recognise and appreciate others.

May we not worry about importance or status. May we trust in our gentleness, and concentrate on doing good.

We pray for those who have died ... Spirit of Jesus, bring them to the festival of God's children, where all is made perfect.

Conclusion
Blessed be God our creator. Blessed be Jesus who gives us hope. Blessed be the Spirit alive among us. Blessed be the Holy Trinity for ever and ever.

Wisdom 9:13-18; Psalm 89; Philemon 9-10, 12-17; Luke 14:25-33

Introduction
As we pray, we ask for the wisdom to be able to understand God's plan and to see where God is leading us.

Prayers
May we experience the joy and happiness of following Jesus. May we give what he asks, and let go of what holds us back.

We pray for people for whom things have turned out badly, and for those who were not able to complete what they started.

We pray for people who are being enslaved – children, women, men. May the world learn to respect all God's children.

Lord, make us know the shortness of life. Concentrate our hearts and energies on what really matters.

We pray for our sisters and brothers who have died … May the dead wake up to a new morning, rejoicing in God's love.

Conclusion
Through these prayers, Lord, grant us the grace to see you more clearly, to love you more dearly, to follow you more nearly, day by day, through Christ our Lord.

Year C Sunday 24 of Ordinary Time

Exodus 32:7-11, 13-14; Psalm 50; 1 Timothy 1:12-17; Luke 15:1-32

Introduction
God loves us with inexhaustible patience. We entrust ourselves to God – our hearts, our hopes, our needs, our prayers.

Prayers
May we share God's joy in welcoming sinners. May we rejoice when people change for the better and turn from sinful ways.

May our church be like God – welcoming rather than judging, including rather than excluding, embracing all who struggle.

We pray for families that have been split up or divided. May bitterness give way to repentance and forgiveness.

We pray for people who give their time to caring for a family member. We hope that they feel appreciated and supported.

We pray for all who have died … Lord, clasp them in your arms and kiss them tenderly, now that they have found their home.

Conclusion
Loving God, give us a pure heart and a contrite spirit, that we may praise you every day. To you be honour and glory for ever and ever.

Amos 8:4-7; Psalm 112; 1 Timothy 2:1-8; Luke 16:1-13

Introduction
Jesus Christ is the link between God and humanity. Through him we now pray, offering our petitions, intercessions and thanksgiving.

Prayers
We pray for those who trample on the needy and oppress the poor. May God turn hearts to the ways of justice and integrity.

We pray for all those among us who work for justice, those who champion the cause of the poor, those who defend the needy.

We have been enlightened by Christ. May we live by the values of the gospel. May we work to create a more equal world.

God wants all people to be saved. We give thanks for the different ways God works in people's hearts, bringing them salvation.

We pray for those who have died ... May they be with God, their deepest desires fulfilled.

Conclusion
We praise you, O God, for your Son Jesus Christ, in whom you love us with an undying love. Glory be ...

Year C Sunday 26 of Ordinary Time

Amos 6:1, 4-7; Psalm 145; 1 Timothy 6:11-16; Luke 16:19-31

Introduction
Your Word, O God, has nourished our spirit. We now put words on the prayers which your Word inspires within us.

Prayers
May we take to heart the message of Jesus – that nobody who dies from human neglect is ever neglected by God.

We pray for those who, in their comfort, do not care about the plight of others.

May each of us play our part in building a world where everybody is treated with equal respect.

We pause quietly for a moment to bring before God our special prayers for ourselves and one another ... *(pause)*

We pray to God for all who have died ... May they rejoice at the Lord's appearing.

Conclusion
Lord, shine light on our path; put hope in our heart; bring fruit to our work. This we ask through Christ our Lord. Amen

Habakkuk 1:2-3; 2:2-4; Psalm 94; 2 Timothy 1:6-8, 13-14; Luke 17:5-10

Introduction
We come before the God who made us, asking God to lead us by the hand, as we pray.

Prayers
We ask God to increase our faith – to give us more trust and less doubt; more courage and less fear.

We pray for people across the world who live in the midst of oppression and outrage, injustice and tyranny, discord and violence.

We pray for all who faithfully fulfil their duties day by day – duties that may be tiring or trying, unrewarding or unnoticed.

May the Lord give us the spirit of power and love and self-control, and make us confident to witness to the good news.

We pray for all who have died ... May God be their salvation.

Conclusion
Lord, you have trusted us to look after something precious. May it grow in our hearts and radiate out into our lives. We ask this through Christ our Lord.

Year C Sunday 28 of Ordinary Time

2 Kings 5:14-17; Psalm 97; 2 Timothy 2:8-13; Luke 17:11-19

Introduction
Our prayers today are prayers of thanks. As we pray, we ask for a spirit of thankfulness to fill the hearts of all God's people.

Prayers
We thank God quietly for all that we have been blessed with in our lives ... *(pause)* May we rejoice in the Lord always.

We thank the Lord for his healing power at work in our lives and our relationships.

Eucharist means thanksgiving. We give thanks for Jesus, given up for our salvation, present among us, source of our hope.

God's news cannot be chained up. We give thanks for all who proclaim the good news. May they bring joy to people's lives.

We pray for our dead ... May they be forever giving thanks and praise in God's presence.

Conclusion
In these and all our prayers we thank you, O God, for the loving kindness you have shown us in Jesus your Son, who is Lord for ever and ever.

Exodus 17:8-13; Psalm 120; 2 Timothy 3:14-4:2; Luke 18:1-8

Introduction
Jesus tells us to never lose heart. We pray now that God will build up our confidence and our courage.

Prayers
We pray for people who are looking for justice and for their just rights. May they not lose heart; may justice be done.

We pray for all who cry to God, day and night. May they find God's help in their cries.

We believe in a God of justice. May God strengthen us to keep working for a just world.

We think of those among us who pray for the rest of us. May God bless them for their faith and their prayer.

We pray for those who have died ... May the Lord guard their coming and going, now and forever.

Conclusion
We praise you, O God, for always listening to our cries and attending to our needs. Glory be ...

Year C Sunday 30 of Ordinary Time

Ecclesiasticus 35:12-14, 16-19; Psalm 32; 2 Timothy 4:6-8, 16-18; Luke 18:9-14

Introduction
We rejoice that God takes notice of us and listens to our pleading. Filled with trust, we bring our prayers before God.

Prayers
May we be humble and not self-righteous. May we know our need of God and open our hearts to God.

We pray for a spirit of mutual respect in society. May people be saved from despising others and looking down on others.

We think of people who are nearing the end of life. May they say with Saint Paul: 'I have fought the fight; I have run the race; I have kept the faith.'

We pray for people who are broken-hearted. We pray for all whose spirit is crushed. May the Lord be close to them.

We pray for all who have died ... May God bring them safely to the heavenly kingdom.

Conclusion
Lord, may our petitions carry to the clouds. May they pierce the clouds and come to you – you whom we bless for ever and ever.

Wisdom 11:22-12:2; Psalm 144; 2 Thessalonians 1:11-2:2; Luke 19:1-10

Introduction
Lord, lover of life, you love all that exists. May these prayers connect us with the power of your love.

Prayers
We pray for people who, like Zacchaeus, are making a determined effort to change for the better.

May our church be a welcoming place. May we rejoice, and not complain, when God is at work in people's hearts.

In a world of greed and ill-gotten wealth, may human hearts be charged with feelings of generosity and solidarity.

Jesus came to stay at Zacchaeus' house. May we all experience the joy of Jesus' presence in our homes.

We pray for all who have died … By God's power, may all their desires for goodness be fulfilled and all the work of their lives be completed.

Conclusion
Loving God, we glorify you and we bless you day after day. We praise your name for ever as we say, Glory be …

Year C Sunday 32 of Ordinary Time

2 Maccabees 7:1-2, 9-14; Psalm 16; 2 Thessalonians 2:16-3:5; Luke 20:27-38

Introduction
We are children of the resurrection, already alive with the new life of Christ. Lord, fill us with hope as we pray.

Prayers
God of the living, may faith in Christ's resurrection give people courage amidst adversity and suffering.

God of the living, help us witness to the resurrection by bringing hope into one another's lives.

God of the living, may people enter into your risen life by loving one another and making the world a more loving place.

God of the living, we praise you for the signs of resurrection in our world. Teach us to see the signs of hope in our midst.

God of the living, we entrust our dead brothers and sisters to you … Fill them, when they awake, with the sight of your glory.

Conclusion
God of new life, we are amazed at your power to transform death into life. May your transforming Spirit renew our souls and renew the world in the image of Jesus, who is Lord for ever and ever.

Malachi 3:19-20; Psalm 97; 2 Thessalonians 3:7-12; Luke 21:5-19

Introduction
Lord, you have called each of us by name, to witness to you. We pray for strength and endurance in our calling.

Prayers
We pray for all who bear witness to the gospel, for all who bear witness to the truth, for all who bear witness to justice.

May God's Spirit give us wisdom and eloquence; may we be strong in standing up for our beliefs.

We pray for people living in the midst of war and revolution. We pray for victims of earthquakes, plague or famine.

May God's light of justice shine out with healing rays for all who suffer innocently and for all who live with integrity.

We pray for all who have died … May they clap their hands and ring out their joy at the presence of the Lord.

Conclusion
God the Father, bathe us in your love. God the Son, inspire us with your passion. God the Spirit, fill us with your courage. Glory be …

Year C Christ the King

2 Samuel 5:1-3; Psalm 121; Colossians 1:12-20; Luke 23:35-43

Introduction
We pray to God, who has taken us out of the power of darkness, and made a place for us in the kingdom of Jesus.

Prayers
We see the power of Christ the King in the weakness of the cross. May his power shine through our weakness.

We pray for all who, like the criminal beside Jesus, are facing capital punishment in different parts of the world.

We pray for all criminals. We pray for all who are in prison. May they know God's love in their hearts.

God wants all to be reconciled in Christ. We pray for all who are enduring conflict or division in their relationships.

We pray for our beloved who have died ... Jesus, remember them as you come into your kingdom.

Conclusion
Dear God, may these prayers help us to grow in love of you. May they help us grow in love of one another. May they help us grow in love of ourselves. We ask this through Christ our Lord.

Feasts and Occasions through the Year

New Year

World Day of Peace

Christian Unity

Presentation of the Lord

World Day of the Sick

Saint Valentine's Day

Saint Patrick

Saint Joseph

Annunciation

Good Friday

Mothers' Day

Fathers Day

Confirmation

First Communion

Examinations

Summer

Birth of John the Baptist

Saints Peter and Paul

Transfiguration

Assumption

Triumph of the Cross

Mission Sunday

All Saints

All Souls

Lateran Basilica

Immaculate Conception

New Year

We thank the Lord for the year just ended, and for being with us in all the joys and sorrows we experienced.

We ask for God's blessing on the year just starting. May we be open and receptive to the many ways in which God will invite us to new life.

We pray quietly for people we know and we offer to God our hopes for them as they begin a new year … *(pause)*

We pray that the year ahead will see God's kingdom coming to birth in a new spirit of solidarity and justice in the world.

World Day of Peace

May the peace and reconciliation achieved by Christ be experienced by people throughout the world in the coming year.

We pray for peace among the religions of the world. May peace among religions be a foundation for peace among all peoples.

May each one of us be an instrument of peace. May our attitudes and words and actions increase the peace in the world.

We pray for all whose lives are dominated by tension and division. May they know the transforming effect of Christ's peace.

We thank the Lord for all the progress made in recent decades and for the new spirit of respect and co-operation among Christians.

We pray for families where there are Christians from different churches. We give thanks for their witness to unity. We ask God's strength for them.

We pray for the different Christian churches in our area. We thank God for our friendship. We ask God to strengthen the bonds between us.

We pray for Christians who find it hard to feel solidarity with one another, and for all who have been hurt by fellow Christians.

We pray that Christians will appreciate how much they share in common. May all Christians work together to proclaim the gospel to the world.

May all Christians find common cause in working together for peace and justice in the world.

May all Christians be united in solidarity with victims of disease or oppression or poverty or war.

As we pray for the unity of all Christians, we also pray with affection for members of other religions.

Presentation of the Lord

Malachi 3:1-4; Psalm 23; Hebrews 2:14-18; Luke 2:22-40

Introduction
In our prayers today, we celebrate the light of Christ in the world, the light that overcomes all darkness.

Prayers
Mary and Joseph presented Jesus in the temple – we pray for parents who present their child for baptism; may God's blessing go with them.

Simeon saw God's salvation – may people who are ageing grow more confident about the meaning of life.

Jesus was presented in the temple – may we all present ourselves to God; may Christ make of us an everlasting gift to God.

We pray for women and men in religious life in different congregations. May they be a witness and a light to the world.

We pray for our dead ... May their eyes see the salvation God has prepared for them.

Conclusion
We lift up our hearts with thanks, for you O Lord have come among us. We lift up our hearts with confidence, for you O Lord can help us. Glory be ...

We pray for all who are sick, who have a special place in Jesus' affections, may they know his compassion in their hearts.

We think of all who care for a family member who is ill or infirm. We hope that they feel appreciated and cared for themselves.

We pray for young girls and boys who are sick. We ask God to give them courage. We pray for their families who love them.

We think of people who are struggling to come to terms with their condition. May they find a new sense of freedom and peace.

We pray for those who are alone in their sickness and do not feel supported or understood.

We think of those with illnesses of the mind. We pray for all who are confused or disoriented or distressed or depressed.

We rejoice with all who are recovering from sickness and we share their gratitude to God the giver of life.

We pray for those who are unable to accept the sickness of one whom they love. May God embrace them in their insecurity.

We hope that people who are sick will continue to minister to those around them, and to be a grace and a light to others.

Saint Valentine's Day

We thank God for love, for how it has brought joy to our lives and helped us to discover ourselves.

We pray that everybody in our community would know that they are lovable and able to love.

We pray that all our communications to each other, whether praise or criticism, be done from a loving heart.

We pray that all who are in love will make that love into something that is deep and steadfast, faithful and life-giving.

We pray for all who have lost the one they loved, that God will be a comforting presence, and encourage them to go on loving.

We pray for loved ones who have died; may they find in God the fullness of the love they tasted on earth.

May our love be modelled on that of Jesus, with a special attention to those who are most in need around us.

We pray for all whose lives are lacking in love; may they not lose heart or become embittered by life.

Jeremiah 1:4-9; Psalm 116; Acts 13:46-49; Luke 10:1-12, 17-20

Introduction
Today we say thanks to God for Saint Patrick and the blessings he has brought to our country.

Prayers
We thank God for all – parents and teachers, witnesses and companions – who have contributed to the shaping of our faith.

May the good news of the gospel touch the hearts of many. We pray for those who have not experienced Christian faith.

We pray for friends and relatives who are living in other parts of the world; may God guide and protect them.

We pray for all the people on our island, that religion will be a force for bringing us together instead of tearing us apart.

May God support all who are reaching out to create a new sense of Christian community and Christian values in our country.

We pray for our children, and we rejoice in the delight and happiness they experience today.

We welcome all who are visiting or returning home for today, and all who have come to make a home in Ireland.

Conclusion
On this special day, we praise and glorify God for Saint Patrick, through whom we have come to know the gospel of Jesus Christ, who is our salvation, now and for ever.
2 Samuel 7:4-5, 12-14, 16; Psalm 88; Romans 4:13, 16-18, 22; Matthew 1:16, 18-21, 24 (or Luke 2:41-51)

Saint Joseph

Introduction
God is Mother; God is Father. On this feast of Joseph, we turn to God our Father, the rock who saves us, the answer to all our prayers.

Prayers
Like Joseph, may we believe and trust in the Lord when believing and trusting are difficult.

Like Joseph, may we not be afraid when God acts in new and unfamiliar ways in our lives.

May parents and their children always trust each other, keep close to each other, and stay in love with each other.

We ask God to bless all fathers and father figures with Joseph's integrity and care. We pray for absent fathers.

We pray for our dead … May they sing forever to the Lord, whose love is unending.

Conclusion
We thank you, loving God, for the gift of Saint Joseph. We ask you to listen to our prayers and to give us a share of his spirit, through Christ our Lord.

Isaiah 7:10-14; 8:10; Psalm 39; Hebrews 10:4-10; Luke 1:26-38

Introduction
In our prayers today we say, 'Here I am, Lord,' and we pray with our hearts the words of the angel to Mary.

Prayers
The angel said, 'Rejoice so highly favoured!' Like Mary, may we feel God's favour and to be happy that God is with us.

The angel said, 'You are to conceive.' Like Mary, may we say 'Yes' and allow Christ into our hearts and lives.

The angel said, 'The Holy Spirit will come upon you.' Like Mary, may we open ourselves to the power of the Spirit.

The angel said, 'Nothing is impossible to God.' Like Mary, may we confidently believe that there is no limit to God's grace.

We pray for our dead ... May the work that God began in them on earth come to completion in heaven.

Conclusion
We rejoice, O Lord, in the good news announced to Mary. May we continue the annunciation, pointing to the good news by the way we live, to the glory of your name, who live for ever and ever.

Good Friday

Introduction
As Jesus dies on the cross,
his arms reach out to embrace all humanity.
In his death, God remembers and embraces
the countless millions of human beings through the centuries
who have lived and died.
They, and we, are part of God forever;
and so we pray for all God's people.

Response:
Some fruit from the tree of your passion fall on us today.

Prayers

For the dead
We pray for those who have died from among ourselves –
mothers or fathers, wives or husbands, sons or daughters,
brothers or sisters, friends or neighbours or relatives.
We bring their faces to mind ... *(pause a few moments)* ...

Lord, we cannot believe that all they meant to us is lost for ever.
At this moment, you share their death;
we wait in confidence that they share your resurrection.

All: Some fruit from the tree of your passion fall on us today.

For people suffering
We pray for all of suffering humanity –
for the poor of the world, often starving;
for innocent victims of crime or catastrophe, war or injustice;
for those who are suffering and those who are dying today –
those we know and those whose faces we will never see –
all who carry a cross ... *(pause)*

318

Lord, you are close to the broken hearted –
you, an innocent victim, a young man in the prime of life.
As you suffer on the cross, take to yourself all who suffer.
May your spirit revive their spirit
that they may continue to hope in you, their Lord and Saviour.

All: Some fruit from the tree of your passion fall on us today.

For all humankind
We pray for all God's people living on this earth –
for people of different colours and races and countries;
for men and women and children in all parts of the world;
for people of different religions and values;
for all who are searching and all who have given up searching …
(pause)

For all our differences, Lord, and all our endless variety,
we all share the same human nature, created in your image.
Teach us to cherish our common humanity,
to think the best and wish the best for every human being.

All: Some fruit from the tree of your passion fall on us today.

For families
We pray for our families, for all parents and children,
for all who are building a community of love
in all kinds of different situations.
We pray for single people and celibate people.
We pray for those who are bereaved
and those who are separated.
We pray for children and adults who have been abandoned …
(pause)

Good Friday

Lord, in your cross we see reflected
the self-giving that is the heart of all families,
all communities of love.
We ask you to bless us from your cross
in all the ups and downs,
joys and struggles of our lives together.
May your cross speak words of hope to us.

All: Some fruit from the tree of your passion fall on us today.

For followers of Christ
We pray for all who follow Christ
in different churches and denominations,
Catholic, Protestant, Orthodox.
We pray for all who are about to be baptised
into these churches.
We pray too for people who are not part of a church
but who have a love for Christ and his teaching … *(pause)*

Lord, on this day, Christians in every part of the world
are united in a common gaze.
As we look together on your cross
look back on us with healing love,
that we may feel the need to be together
in continuing your mission.

All: Some fruit from the tree of your passion fall on us today.

For our church
We pray for our own Catholic Church
and we think of the challenges it faces today.
We pray for all its members, men and women,
richer and poorer, younger and older.
We pray for [ ] our Pope and [ ] our bishop… *(pause)*

On this sacred day, Lord, you open our souls,
you show us our inner hearts.
May the grace of your death reach deep down into your church
and touch it at its inner core.
May your church be your faithful witness,
humble in itself, but strong and confident in you.

All: Some fruit from the tree of your passion fall on us today.

For the powerful of the world
We pray for the powerful people in our world,
the people with wealth, the people with political power,
who have such control over the life and destiny of others,
often without realising it.
We pray for the leaders of our own country
and all among us with political or economic power … *(pause)*

In your cross, Lord, we see the weakness of God,
weakness more powerful than power.
Teach us the power of weakness; teach us to use power well –
for happiness and not just for prosperity,
for good and not just for gain,
for building solidarity rather than division.

All: Some fruit from the tree of your passion fall on us today.

Good Friday

For our local community
We pray for our local community –
the neighbours we know and those who are strangers to us.
We pray for our young people and for our older people.
We pray for all who are building community.
We pray for all who are alone and seeking community ... *(pause)*

Your death on the cross, Lord, was your final gift to life.
Teach us the lesson of your cross,
that life is lived most fully when we live for one another –
when we build the kind of life together
that you lived and died for.

All: Some fruit from the tree of your passion fall on us today.

Conclusion
(Old Irish prayer)
O King of the Friday,
whose limbs were stretched on the cross;
O Lord who did suffer
the bruises, the wounds and the loss;
we stretch ourselves
beneath the shield of your might;
some fruit from the tree of your passion
fall on us this night.

Mother's Day

Today is Mothers' Day and we rejoice with all mothers in the love they have for their families.

May God bless all mothers and give them peace in their hearts.

We reach out with our prayers to mothers who are struggling or overburdened, anxious or afraid.

We pray for those who are soon to become mothers. May God be with them in this new moment in their lives.

We pray for our own mothers. We thank them for our existence; we bless them for their love.

We pray for mothers who have died. May we share joy with them again in our heavenly home.

Fathers' Day

Today is fathers' day and we rejoice with all fathers in the love they have for their family.

We ask God to bless all fathers with caring, loving hearts.

We pray to God to be with all fathers who are overburdened or struggling in any way.

We pray for those who are soon to become fathers. May God be with them in this new moment in their lives.

We pray for our own fathers. We thank them for our existence; we bless them for their love.

We pray for fathers who have died. May we share joy with them again in our heavenly home.

Confirmation

We pray for the boys and girls who make their Confirmation this year …

May they always feel treasured and lovable.

May God bless them on their journey of faith.

May they live like Jesus and play their part in making the world a better place.

We thank God for the Spirit that is in them, for the goodness in their hearts, for the kindness in their thoughts, for the love in their actions.

May God's Spirit be alive in them, bearing fruit in love and joy, generosity and gentleness.

We pray for their families …

May God bless their families with harmony and happiness.

May each of our families be a community of care and of prayer.

We pray for all of us in our parish family …

May the grace of Confirmation move us to play our part in the care of our parish community.

May God's Spirit give us confidence in how gifted we are and help to use our gifts for the good of all.

We pray for the boys and girls who make their First Communion this year …

May they delight in how loved and special they are.

May God bless them on their journey of faith.

May they always feel close to Jesus as their special friend.

May going to Mass and Communion always feel special for them.

As they grow up, may their individual gifts come to light and may their personalities flower.

We pray for their families …

May God bless their families with harmony and happiness.

May each of our families be a place of caring for each other and praying together.

We pray for all of us in our parish family …

May we grow more and more aware of ourselves as the Body of Christ, joined together in a spiritual bond in Christ.

May the Eucharist we celebrate make a difference to our lives. As we live the Eucharist, may we make a difference to the lives of others.

Examinations

We reach out with our prayers, to all amongst us who are doing exams or preparing for exams. We are with them in their efforts, in their hopes and in their anxiety. We hope that they do well.

We pray for all families where there are people doing exams. May the family be a place of support and of calm.

Examination Results

We reach out in our prayer to all who are getting their examination results around now. We rejoice with those who do well. We share the disappointment of those who don't do so well. We wish each one of them the best in the year ahead.

We pray for all who are making decisions and choices about their future. May their decisions be wise. May their choices be courageous.

Start of Summer

May the Lord bless us as Summer begins. May it be a happy time for all. We pray for families, that Summer will be a special time and bring them close together.

We welcome those who are here among us on holiday. May our time together be happy and relaxing.

We pray that holiday time will be a time of fun and relaxation.

May our children enjoy their holidays, and may grown-ups have a chance to stand back and be refreshed.

We pray for all who are travelling during the holidays; may they be safe and have a good time.

End of Summer

As the Summer holidays come to an end, we say thanks to God for the fun they brought and for the time together.

We pray for our children going back to school. We pray for the boys and girls who are starting school. We ask God to bless all parents.

We think of all for whom September marks a new start – at study, at work, at home –we ask God to bless us with the grace of new beginnings.

We thank God for the joy of life, for the people we love, for the memories we create, for all that there is to look forward to.

Birth of John the Baptist

Isaiah 49:1-6; Psalm 138; Acts 13:22-26; Luke 1:57-66,80
(Vigil: Jeremiah 1:4-10; Psalm 70; 1 Peter 1:8-12; Luke 1:5-17)

Introduction
In our prayers today, we ask for ourselves a share of the spirit that the Lord gave to John the Baptist.

Prayers
May the birth of John the Baptist help us to appreciate the wonder of our being and the wonder of our calling.

May our own children be a joy and a delight – may they be courageous people, with loving hearts and prophetic voices.

May God continue to raise up people like John the Baptist, single-mindedly serving the truth and speaking prophetically.

We praise God for all the people in our lives and in our world who, like John the Baptist, point the way to Christ.

We pray for our dead ... May they be filled with a joy so glorious that it cannot be described.

Conclusion
Loving God, we offer our prayers in faith and love of you, through Christ our Lord.

*Acts 12:1-11; Psalm 33; 2 Timothy 4:6-8, 17-18; Matthew 16:13-19
(Vigil: Acts 3:1-10; Psalm 18; Galatians 1:11-20; John 21:15-19)*

Introduction
In our prayers today, we ask for ourselves a share of the spirit that the Lord gave to Peter and Paul.

Prayers
May we, like Peter and Paul, be amazed at what the Lord is doing in our lives.

May the Lord work through us, as he did through Peter and Paul. Through our witness, may others come to know the Lord.

May the Lord raise up people in today's church, like Peter and Paul, with the vision and faith to guide us into the future.

May today's church be blessed by Peter and Paul – with the freshness of their faith and the energy of their mission.

We pray for our dead … Lord, bring them safely to your heavenly kingdom.

Conclusion
In these and all our prayers we praise you, O God, for the goodness you have shown us in Christ our Lord.

The Transfiguration of the Lord

Daniel 7:9-10, 13-14; Psalm 96; 2 Peter 1:16-19; Matthew 17:1-9 (year A) /Mark 9:2-10 (year B) /Luke 9:28-36 (year C)

Introduction

We turn to God, whose glory is revealed to us in Christ the Lord, and we confidently open our hearts in prayer.

Prayers

We thank God for moments in life when our eyes are opened and we see things more clearly.

May we grow to appreciate the wonder of God in the ordinary events and encounters of our daily life.

We pray for all who are going through struggles and dark times, that faith in Jesus the Lord will sustain them.

May we make time for silence and prayer in our lives, where we can be still and aware of the presence of God.

We pray for our dead ... May a new day dawn on them and may the morning star rise in their hearts.

Conclusion

We ask you, Lord, to listen to our prayers, to show us your majesty, and to lead us to the fullness of your glory, where you live for ever and ever.

Revelation 11:19; 12:1-6, 10; Psalm 44; 1 Corinthians 15:20-26; Luke 1:39-56
(Vigil: 1 Chronicles 15:3-4, 15-16; 16:1-2; Psalm 131; 1Corinthians 15:54-57; Luke 11:27-28)

Introduction
On this feast we rejoice that Mary, the first of all the disciples, is united with Christ in heaven, and we pray.

Prayers
We give thanks for the assurance that this feast brings; that where Mary has gone, we too may follow.

As Mary is united with Jesus in heaven, may we all one day be reunited with our departed family and friends.

We pray to be inspired by the faith of Mary. May we, like her, bring Christ into the world.

May God, who exalted Mary in her lowliness, be the hope of all who are bowed down, and the strength of all who are humble.

We pray for all who have died … May they be escorted with gladness and joy into the palace of the Lord.

Conclusion
With Mary, we proclaim the greatness of the Lord, the holiness of the Lord's name, and the power of the Lord in our midst. Glory be …

The Triumph of the Cross

Numbers 21:4-9; Psalm 77; Philippians 2:6-11; John 3:13-17

Introduction
We rejoice in the words of today's gospel, 'God so loved the world that he sent his only Son'; and we bring our prayers to the One who loves us so much.

Prayers
May Jesus, who died on the cross for us, give us patience and hope when things are hard.

We pray for people who don't know God's love. May they feel the love flowing from the cross to touch each human heart.

We pray for people carrying a cross – of worry or fear, of grief or loss, of pain or failure. May God's power lift them up.

We thank God for mothers and fathers, and for all who empty themselves for the sake of serving others.

We pray for our dead ... May Jesus, lifted up on the cross, lift them up to enjoy eternal life with him.

Conclusion
As we offer these prayers, we bend our knees at the name of Jesus and we proclaim with our tongues that he is Lord, to the glory of God the Father, forever and ever.

Introduction

Today we pray about 'mission' – God's mission in sending Jesus to us; and our call to be God's missionaries in the world.

Prayers

We praise God for the people through whom we have heard the good news of the gospel – we pause to think of God's missionaries to ourselves.

We praise God for the many ways in which people communicate to each other the love of God – missionaries without knowing it.

We praise God whose Spirit is at work in each of us, enabling us to bring hope to others – enabling us to be missionaries.

We ask God to enthuse the church with a new feeling of mission, to reach out with the good news of the gospel to today's world.

We ask God to bless all who go to serve abroad out of a sense of mission to their fellow human beings.

We pray for all who have died ... May the good news of the gospel fill them with an overflowing joy.

Conclusion

In our prayers, we give thanks and praise for God's mission to us, in sending Jesus and in sending the Spirit, drawing us into God's own life, now and for ever.

All Saints

Revelation 7:2-4, 9-14; Psalm 23; 1 John 3:1-3; Matthew 5:1-12

Introduction
Our prayers today join us, who are the living saints, with all the saints who have gone before us into God's presence.

Prayers
We recall the saints we are named after, and we recall the inspirational figures in our lives – saints living and dead.

We thank God for the mystery of what we are – part of the communion of saints, that spans heaven and earth.

The saints in heaven pray with us. We rely on them as we pray quietly, for ourselves, for each other, for the world … *(pause)*

Those who have gone before us endured all the ups and downs of life; may their memory increase our courage and give us hope.

As a communion of saints, we pray; may what each of us does, and what each of us suffers, bear fruit for the good of all.

Conclusion
The saints in heaven praise you for ever, O Lord. We echo their song of praise as we say, Glory be …

We remember our own dead and our own sadness ... Tears speak out our grief, but they also witness to our love and we are glad to have loved so much that we can cry. May those we have loved rest in your embrace, O Lord.

We remember the loss and grief of others around us. We think of the funerals we have been at in the last year ... We pray especially for those who are without consolation.

We pray for all the people who have died in our community and in our country this past year – older people; younger people; those who died content; those who died struggling – all sharing in common that they died into the arms of our loving God.

Wherever there is grief, may hope be allowed to enter in and sit beside it, as its silent companion. May we learn to believe what we cannot see, that our life is hidden with Christ in God.

We pray for all who have died around the world in the last year. We pray for those who have starved to death; for those who were victims of natural disasters; for those who were killed by their fellow human beings. We pray, knowing that you, Lord, have carved their names on the palm of your hand.

We know that each person dies just as they are. We ask you, Lord, to work through our prayers, for the forgiveness of their faults, the purification of their souls and the completion of their journey into the arms of your everlasting love.

As we remember the dead today, may it teach us to see life in true perspective. May we live life truly and wisely, graciously and generously. May we not be afraid of death, but may we grow to hope, heartened by the way in which you, O Lord, are constantly bringing life out of death and light out of darkness.

Lateran Basilica

Ezekiel 47:1-2, 8-9, 12; Psalm 45; 1 Corinthians 3:9-11, 16-17; John 2:13-22

Introduction
We pray today, together with Pope [ ] the Bishop of Rome, for the church throughout the world, that it will be a source of life for the world.

Prayers
May the church be a life-giving presence – may the good news of the gospel permeate as living water into all parts of society.

May we grow in our sense of what we are as 'church' – that we are God's temple, where God's Spirit dwells.

May the word 'church' mean more than a building – may people find it to be a welcoming community, alive with God's Spirit.

We pray for all who are involved in planning for the church of tomorrow – bless them Lord with courage and vision.

We pray for our dead … We pray with confidence that you, O God, raise them up to a share in Christ's risen life.

Conclusion
May all that we say and all that we do be built on the foundation of Jesus Christ, the cornerstone of our faith and our lives, who lives and reigns for ever and ever.

Genesis 3:9-15, 20; Psalm 97; Ephesians 1:3-6, 11-12; Luke 1:26-38

Introduction
Today we celebrate the words, 'Hail Mary full of grace', and we pray with thanks for the grace that is at the heart of the universe.

Prayers
May today's feast teach us that, deeper than any sin or failure, we are graced at the core of our being.

Like Mary, may our minds be filled with the truth of Christ, and our hearts with his love, so that Christ may be born in our lives.

We thank God that grace is stronger than sin. May we rely on the power of grace to protect us from sin and evil.

We pray for our world and its people; may all enjoy what we celebrate today – freedom from the power of sin.

We pray for our dead... We ask you, Lord, who chose them before the world was made, to bring them to your presence.

Conclusion
Today, we pray with Mary, our hearts amazed by what God can do in our lives. Glory be ...

Prayers for the Dead

*These are the collated intercessions for the dead
from the above sets of prayers of the faithful.
See also the prayers for Good Friday and for All Souls.*

May they awake to eternal day in the sight of God.

May they praise you, O Lord, and sing to your name.

May there be everlasting joy on their faces.

May 'Emmanuel – God is with us' be their joyful refrain forever.

May they be blessed for ever as members of God's family.

May they experience in full the new life of baptism.

May they join with all the saints in glorifying God for ever.

May they see the Lord's goodness and savour the Lord's sweet-ness in the land of the living.

May they rejoice in all the happiness and blessings of God's kingdom.

We entrust them to God, who is faithful from age to age and from life to death.

May they enjoy completely the divine grace that comes to us as an abundant free gift.

May they live a new life with the risen Christ.

May God who raised Jesus from the dead breathe resurrection life into them.

May the seed of divine life come to full flower in God's king-dom.

May their faults be burned away. May their goodness shine like the sun in God's kingdom.

May they come to share God's own glory.

May there be nothing now between them and the love of Christ.

After the storms and struggles of life, may they experience the calm of God's peace.

May the faith they had in life find its fulfilment in God's presence.

May they adore and glorify God forever.

May they praise God with joy. May they rejoice and be filled at God's banquet.

May they see the face of God and live.

May the Lord crown them with love and compassion.

Lord we know that alive or dead, we belong to you.

May Christ be glorified in all who have died.

May they praise God's name for ever.

We ask God to raise them high, to joyfully acclaim that Jesus is Lord.

May they rejoice for ever in the communion of saints.

In the Lord's own house may they dwell for ever and ever.

May they sing a new song to the Lord, full of worship and praise.

May they know the fullness of love in God's presence.

Guard their souls in peace before you O Lord.

May God give them new life in Jesus.

They are children of the light. May Christ bring them to everlasting day.

In the Lord's own house may they dwell for ever and ever.

We look forward to Christ's coming in glory, when all will be united in him forever.

We ask you, Lord, to gather them in your arms and hold them against your breast.

May they glorify the Lord for ever.

May they sing for ever of your love, O Lord.

May they be blessed for ever as members of God's family.

We pray with confidence that God delights in them forever.

May there be a new song in their mouths, praising and delight-ing in God.

May they share in all the joy of God's kingdom.

May the Lord lead them by the hand to the place of perfect peace.

May they be fully reconciled in God's love.

May their souls be filled as with a banquet. May their mouths praise God with joy.

May they have the fullness of life, and happiness in God's pres-ence for ever.

May they be made altogether new in the Lord.

May they enjoy perfect peace in the presence of God.

May our prayer find them enjoying the vision of God's glory.

May the Lord bring them to the light of eternal day.

May they be renewed in the image of their creator. May they be revealed in all their glory.

May they ring out their joy to the Lord.

May they know the joy that Jesus came to share with us.

May they take their place at the feast in God's kingdom.

Spirit of Jesus, bring them to the city of the living God, to the festival of God's children, where all is made perfect.

May the dead wake up to a new morning, rejoicing and filled with God's love.

Lord, clasp them in your arms and kiss them tenderly, now that they have found their home.

May they rejoice at the Lord's Appearing.

May God be their salvation.

May they be forever giving thanks and praise in God's presence.

May the Lord guard their coming and going, now and forever.

May God bring them safely to the heavenly kingdom.

By God's power, may all their desires for goodness be fulfilled and all the work of their lives be completed.

Fill them, when they awake, with the sight of your glory.

May they clap their hands and ring out their joy at the presence of the Lord.

Jesus, remember them as you come into your kingdom.

Let us be glad that they are ringing out their joy to the Lord.

May they share with Mary in glorifying God for ever.

May they experience all the spiritual blessings of heaven.

Gladden them, O Lord, with the light of your face.

As Mary is united with Jesus in heaven, may we all one day be reunited with our departed family and friends.

May God raise their heads in glory.

May they see what no eye has seen; may they enjoy all that God has prepared for them.

May they know how great is God's healing and saving power.

May they ring out their joy in the company of all the saints.

May they be with the Lord, forever singing God's praises.

May they rejoice and be happy at God's heavenly banquet.

May they experience perfect peace and reconciliation in God's presence.

May their souls be still and may they rest in God.

May Christ who has entered heaven lead them to God.

May they enjoy the vision of the glory of Christ.

May they rejoice in the wonder of God's glory.

May they find in God that which is more desirable than anything else.

May they be at peace, their hopes fulfilled in the vision of God's glory.

May they be raised up with Christ and share a place with God in heaven.

May they dwell in the Lord's own house for ever and ever.

May Jesus, risen from the dead, draw them to himself.

May God raise them from their graves and give life to their mortal bodies.

May they enjoy completely the new life that comes from the cross.

May Christ the morning star bring them the light of life and open everlasting day.

May Christ in his passion and death lead them to new life.

May they enjoy the love that has no end.

May they come into an inheritance that can never fade away.

Lift up the light of your face on them, O Lord.

May their hearts rejoice and their souls be glad; may their bodies rest in safety.

Show them the path of life, the fulness of joy in your presence, and happiness at your right hand for ever.

May they be like God, seeing God as God really is.

May they dwell for ever in the Lord's own house; may their cup be overflowing.

May they live for ever, with joy in their hearts.

May their faces be radiant with the light of Christ's glory.

May our prayers accompany them to the place that Jesus has prepared for them.

May they sing a new song to the Lord and be full of joy.

In heaven may they have the completeness of the love they experienced on earth.

May they enter the everlasting home built for us by God.

May God, who raised Jesus to life, raise them with Jesus and place them by his side.

May they hear the words of Jesus, 'You will see me, because I live, and you will live'.

We pray that they are in God's presence and enjoying God's presence completely.

May they flourish for ever, making their home with the Lord.

Send forth your Spirit, O Lord, and bring them to their inheritance as your cherished children.

Let your face shine on them, O Lord, and take them to your heart.

May God's coming to them be as certain as the dawn and as refreshing as spring rains watering the earth.

May the Holy Spirit bring them to Christ, to share in his glory as children of God.

May they feast with unending joy at the heavenly banquet.

May they know the love of Christ and be filled with the utter fulness of God.

We pray that God will lead them to the haven they desire.

May God, who wants all to live, raise them up.

May they be for ever amazed at the vision of God's glory.

May God bless them with all the spiritual blessings of heaven.

May their spirits overflow with gladness at the banquet of the Lord.

May they see your glory, O Lord, and may they rejoice in you as you rejoice in them.

We ask the Lord to gladden their hearts and to give light to their eyes.

May they thank you, O Lord, as they delight in the abundant blessings of heaven.

May they see the Lord face to face and know the love that has no end.

May they bless the Lord before the angels and sing for ever to God's glory.

May a new day dawn on them and may the morning star rise in their hearts.

May God bring them to that holy land where they will never hunger or thirst again.

May their hopes be fulfilled as they share in Christ's rising from the dead.

May their spirits be transformed in the image of the risen Lord.

May they look towards the Lord and be radiant.

May they be escorted with gladness and joy into the palace of the Lord.

May their dying be swallowed up in victory and may they know that they did not labour in vain.

May they live in perfect bliss, their beings transformed by God's undying love.

May they praise the Lord, who raises our souls from the dead.

May they lack no blessing as they share in the heavenly banquet.

May the Spirit of the Lord give them eternal life.

In the presence of God, may everything be good for them, everything perfect.

May they be happy for ever, looking on God's face and singing God's praise.

May God, who keeps faith for ever, open their eyes and may they sing for joy.

May they receive the blessing that comes with the appearing of our Saviour Jesus Christ.

May they walk in the presence of the Lord in the land of the living.

May Jesus, lifted up on the cross, lift them up to enjoy eternal life with him.

May God, who has been with them in life and in death, give them glory.

Lord, uphold their lives and save them by your name.

May they enjoy the Lord's friendship and dwell in perfect peace.

May their eyes see the salvation God has prepared for them.

May the radiance of God's glory bring absolute joy to them.

May they reach the perfect goodness which Christ produces in us for the glory of God.

May the risen Christ bring them to the love that has no end.

May the Lord one day reunite us with those who have died, never to be separated again.

May they shout with joy and rejoice with all their hearts.

May they sing forever to the Lord, whose love is unending.

Lord, raise their souls from the dead and restore them to life.

May the work that God began in them on earth come to completion in heaven.

Lord, bring them safely to your heavenly kingdom.

May they be filled with a joy so glorious that it cannot be described.

We pray with confidence that you, O God, raise them up to a share in Christ's risen life.

We ask you, Lord, who chose them before the world was made, to bring them to live through love in your presence.

Lord, shine your glory on them and amaze them with your love.

May they be blessed, as the promises made to them by the Lord are fulfilled.

May they come before the Lord, singing for joy.

May they see the light of God and be content.

May the good news of the gospel fill them with an overflowing joy.

May the Lord transfigure their bodies into copies of his glorious body.

May they enter into God's own home, where there is no more mourning or sadness.

May the Lord comfort them and lead them to streams of living water.

May the Lord bring them to the promised land, where they will know only love and joy.

May they come to the holy city, lit by the radiant glory of God, and be enthralled.

May they rejoice and be completely happy in God.

May they look towards the Lord and be radiant.

May Jesus, the bright star of morning, bring them to everlasting day.

May they come to the complete experience of God's love.

May they enjoy a gladness even greater than we can imagine.

May Christ appear with salvation to those who are waiting for him.

May they be with Jesus this day in Paradise.

May they shine as bright as stars for all eternity.

May they reach the prize that God calls us to receive in Christ.

May they know the incomparable happiness of seeing God.

Index of Scripture References

*No liturgical year is included in the reference
if the reading is used for the feast in all three years.
The prayers do not necessarily incorporate
themes from every reading every Sunday.*

Old Testament
Genesis 1:1-2:2. Easter Vigil.
Genesis 2:7-9; 3:1-7. Year A, Lent 1.
Genesis 2:18-24. Year B, Sunday 27.
Genesis 3:9-15. Year B, Sunday 10.
Genesis 3:9-15,20. Immaculate Conception.
Genesis 9:8-15. Year B, Lent 1.
Genesis 11:1-9. Pentecost.
Genesis 12:1-4. Year A, Lent 2.
Genesis 14:18-20. Year C, Body and Blood of Christ.
Genesis 15:1-6; 21:1-3. Year B, Holy Family.
Genesis 15:5-12,17-18. Year C, Lent 2.
Genesis 18:1-10. Year C, Sunday 16.
Genesis 18:20-32. Year C, Sunday 17.
Genesis 22:1-2,9-13,15-18. Year B, Lent 2.
Genesis 22:1-18. Easter Vigil.

Exodus 3:1-8,13-15. Year C, Lent 3.
Exodus 12:1-8,11-14. Holy Thursday.
Exodus 14:15-15:1. Easter Vigil.
Exodus 15. Easter Vigil.
Exodus 16:2-4. Year B, Sunday 18.
Exodus 17:3-7. Year A, Lent 3.
Exodus 17:8-13. Year C, Sunday 29.
Exodus 19:2-6. Year A, Sunday 11.
Exodus 19:3-8,16-20. Pentecost.
Exodus 20:1-17. Year B, Lent 3.
Exodus 22:20-26. Year A, Sunday 30.
Exodus 24:3-8. Year B, Body and Blood of Christ.
Exodus 32:7-11,13-14. Year C, Sunday 24.
Exodus 34:4-6,8-9. Year A, Trinity.

Leviticus 13:1-2,44-46. Year B, Sunday 6.
Leviticus 19:1-2,17-18. Year A, Sunday 7.

Numbers 6:22-27. Mary Mother of God.
Numbers 11:25-29. Year B, Sunday 26.
Numbers 21:4-9. Triumph of the Cross.

Deuteronomy 4:1-2,6-8. Year B, Sunday 22.
Deuteronomy 4:32-34,39-40. Year B, Trinity.
Deuteronomy 5:12-15. Year B, Sunday 9.
Deuteronomy 6:2-6. Year B, Sunday 31.

Psalm 17. Year A, Sunday 30; Year B, Sunday 31.

Psalm 18. Easter Vigil; Saints Peter and Paul; Year B, Lent 3; Year B, Sunday 26; Year C, Sunday 3; Year C, Sunday 15.

Psalm 21. Year B, Easter 5.

Psalm 22. Palm Sunday; Year A, Lent 4; Year A, Easter 4; Year A, Sunday 28; Year A, Christ the King; Year B, Sunday 16; Year C, Sacred Heart.

Psalm 23. Presentation of the Lord; All Saints; Year A, Advent 4

Psalm 24. Year A, Sunday 26; Year B, Lent 1; Year B, Sunday 3; Year C, Advent 1.

Psalm 26. Year A, Easter 7; Year A, Sunday 3; Year C, Lent 2.

Psalm 28. Year A, Baptism of the Lord.

Psalm 29. Easter Vigil; Year B, Sunday 13; Year C, Easter 3; Year C, Sunday 10.

Psalm 30. Year A, Sunday 9.

Psalm 31. Year B, Sunday 6; Year C, Sunday 11.

Psalm 32. Easter Vigil; Year A, Easter 5; Year A, Lent 2; Year B, Trinity; Year B, Sunday 29; Year C, Sunday 19; Year C, Sunday 30.

Psalm 33. Saints Peter and Paul; Year B, Sunday 19; Year B, Sunday 20; Year B, Sunday 21; Year C, Lent 4.

Psalm 39. Annunciation; Year A, Sunday 2; Year B, Sunday 2; Year C, Sunday 20.

Psalm 40. Year B, Sunday 7.

Psalm 41. Easter Vigil.

Psalm 44. Assumption.

Psalm 45. Lateran Basilica.

Psalm 46. Ascension.

Psalm 49. Year A, Sunday 10.

Psalm 50. Ash Wednesday; Easter Vigil; Year A, Lent 1; Year B, Lent 5; Year C, Sunday 24.

Psalm 53. Year B, Sunday 25.

Psalm 61. Year A, Sunday 8.

Psalm 62. Year A, Sunday 22; Year A, Sunday 32; Year C, Sunday 12.

Psalm 64. Year A, Sunday 15.

Psalm 65. Year A, Easter 6; Year C, Sunday 14.

Psalm 66. Year A, Sunday 20; Year C, Easter 6; Mary Mother of God.

Psalm 67. Year C, Sunday 22.

Psalm 68. Year A, Sunday 12; Year C, Sunday 15.

Psalm 70. Birth of John the Baptist; Year C, Sunday 4.

Psalm 71. Epiphany; Year A, Advent 2.

Psalm 77. Triumph of the Cross; Year B, Sunday 18.

Psalm 79. Year A, Sunday 27; Year B, Advent 1; Year C, Advent 4.

Psalm 80. Year B, Sunday 9.

Psalm 83. Year C, Holy Family.

Psalm 84. Year A, Sunday 19; Year B, Advent 2; Year B, Sunday 15.

Psalm 145. Year A, Advent 3; Year A, Sunday 4; Year B, Sunday 23; Year B, Sunday 32; Year C, Sunday 26.
Psalm 146. Year B, Sunday 5.
Psalm 147. Second Sunday after Christmas; Year A, Body and Blood of Christ.

Proverbs 8:22-31. Year C, Trinity.
Proverbs 9:1-6. Year B, Sunday 20.
Proverbs 31:10-13,19-20,30-31. Year A, Sunday 33.

Ecclesiastes 1:2; 2:21-23. Year C, Sunday 18.

Isaiah 2:1-5. Year A, Advent 1.
Isaiah 5:1-7. Year A, Sunday 27.
Isaiah 6:1-8. Year C, Sunday 5.
Isaiah 7:10-14. Year A, Advent 4.
Isaiah 7:10-14; 8:10. Annunciation.
Isaiah 8:29-9:3. Year A, Sunday 3.
Isaiah 9:1-7. Christmas, Midnight.
Isaiah 11:1-10. Year A, Advent 2.
Isaiah 12. Easter Vigil.
Isaiah 12:2-6. Year B, Baptism of the Lord; Year B, Sacred Heart; Year C, Advent 3.
Isaiah 22:19-23. Year A, Sunday 21.
Isaiah 25:6-10. Year A, Sunday 28.
Isaiah 35:1-6,10. Year A, Advent 3.
Isaiah 35:4-7. Year B, Sunday 23.
Isaiah 40:1-5,9-11. Year B, Advent 2; Year C, Baptism of the Lord.
Isaiah 42:1-4,6-7. Year A, Baptism of the Lord.
Isaiah 43:16-21. Year C, Lent 5.
Isaiah 43:18-19,21-22,24-25. Year B, Sunday 7.
Isaiah 45:1,4-6. Year A, Sunday 29.
Isaiah 49:1-6. Birth of John the Baptist.
Isaiah 49:3,5-6. Year A, Sunday 2.
Isaiah 49:14-15. Year A, Sunday 8.
Isaiah 50:4-7. Palm Sunday.
Isaiah 50:5-9. Year B, Sunday 24.
Isaiah 52:7-10. Christmas, Day.
Isaiah 53:10-11. Year B, Sunday 29.
Isaiah 54:5-14. Easter Vigil.
Isaiah 55:1-3. Year A, Sunday 18.
Isaiah 55:1-11. Easter Vigil; Year B, Baptism of the Lord.
Isaiah 55:6-9. Year A, Sunday 25.
Isaiah 55:10-11. Year A, Sunday 15.

Amos 6:1,4-7. Year C, Sunday 26.
Amos 7:12-15. Year B, Sunday 15.
Amos 8:4-7. Year C, Sunday 25.

Jonah 3:1-5,10. Year B, Sunday 3.

Micah 5:1-4. Year C, Advent 4.

Habakkuk 1:2-3; 2:2-4. Year C, Sunday 27.

Zephaniah 2:3; 3:12-13. Year A, Sunday 4.
Zephaniah 3:14-18. Year C, Advent 3.

Zechariah 9:9-10. Year A, Sunday 14.
Zechariah 12:10-11. Year C, Sunday 12.

Malachi 1:14-2:2, 8-10. Year A, Sunday 31.
Malachi 3:1-4. Presentation of the Lord.
Malachi 3:19-20. Year C, Sunday 33.

Wisdom 1:13-15; 2:23-24. Year B, Sunday 13.
Wisdom 2:12,17-20. Year B, Sunday 25.
Wisdom 6:12-16. Year A, Sunday 32.
Wisdom 7:7-11. Year B, Sunday 28.
Wisdom 9:13-18. Year C, Sunday 23.
Wisdom 11:22-12:2. Year C, Sunday 31.
Wisdom 12:13,16-19. Year A, Sunday 16.
Wisdom 18:6-9. Year C, Sunday 19.

Ecclesiasticus 3:2-6,12-14. Year A, Holy Family.
Ecclesiasticus 3:17-20,28-29. Year C, Sunday 22.
Ecclesiasticus 15:15-20. Year A, Sunday 6.
Ecclesiasticus 24:1-2,8-12. Second Sunday after Christmas.
Ecclesiasticus 27:4-7. Year C, Sunday 8.
Ecclesiasticus 27:30-28:7. Year A, Sunday 24.
Ecclesiasticus 35:12-14,16-19. Year C, Sunday 30.

Baruch 3:9-15,32-4:4. Easter Vigil.
Baruch 5:1-9. Year C, Advent 2.

2 Maccabees 7:1-2,9-14. Year C, Sunday 32.

New Testament
Matthew 1:1-25. Christmas, Vigil.
Matthew 1:16,18-21,24. Saint Joseph.
Matthew 1:18-24. Year A, Advent 4.
Matthew 2:1-12. Epiphany.

Matthew 25:31-46. Year A, Christ the King.
Matthew 26:14-27:66. Year A, Palm Sunday.
Matthew 28:1-10. Year A, Easter Vigil.
Matthew 28:16-20. Year A, Ascension; Year B, Trinity.

Mark 1:1-8. Year B, Advent 2.
Mark 1:7-11. Year B, Baptism of the Lord.
Mark 1:12-15. Year B, Lent 1.
Mark 1:14-20. Year B, Sunday 3.
Mark 1:21-28. Year B, Sunday 4.
Mark 1:29-39. Year B, Sunday 5.
Mark 1:40-45. Year B, Sunday 6.
Mark 2:1-12. Year B, Sunday 7.
Mark 2:18-22. Year B, Sunday 8.
Mark 2:23-3:6. Year B, Sunday 9.
Mark 3:20-35. Year B, Sunday 10.
Mark 4:26-34. Year B, Sunday 11.
Mark 4:35-41. Year B, Sunday 12.
Mark 5:21-43. Year B, Sunday 13.
Mark 6:1-6. Year B, Sunday 14.
Mark 6:7-13. Year B, Sunday 15.
Mark 6:30-34. Year B, Sunday 16.
Mark 7:1-8,14-15,21-23. Year B, Sunday 22.
Mark 7:31-37. Year B, Sunday 23.
Mark 8:27-35. Year B, Sunday 24.
Mark 9:2-10. Year B, Lent 2; Year B, Transfiguration.
Mark 9:30-37. Year B, Sunday 25.
Mark 9:38-43,45,47-48. Year B, Sunday 26.
Mark 10:2-16. Year B, Sunday 27.
Mark 10:17-30. Year B, Sunday 28.
Mark 10:35-45. Year B, Sunday 29.
Mark 10:46-52. Year B, Sunday 30.
Mark 11:1-10. Year B, Palm Sunday.
Mark 12:28-34. Year B, Sunday 31.
Mark 12:38-44. Year B, Sunday 32.
Mark 13:24-32. Year B, Sunday 33.
Mark 13:33-37. Year B, Advent 1.
Mark 14:1-15:47. Year B, Palm Sunday.
Mark 14:12-16,22-26. Year B, Body and Blood of Christ.
Mark 16:1-7. Year B, Easter Vigil.
Mark 16:15-20. Year B, Ascension.

Luke 15:1-3,11-32. Year C, Lent 4.
Luke 15:1-32. Year C, Sunday 24.
Luke 15:3-7. Year C, Sacred Heart.
Luke 16:1-13. Year C, Sunday 25.
Luke 16:19-31. Year C, Sunday 26.
Luke 17:5-10. Year C, Sunday 27.
Luke 17:11-19. Year C, Sunday 28.
Luke 18:1-8. Year C, Sunday 29.
Luke 18:9-14. Year C, Sunday 30.
Luke 19:1-10. Year C, Sunday 31.
Luke 19:28-40. Year C, Palm Sunday.
Luke 20:27-38. Year C, Sunday 32.
Luke 21:5-19. Year C, Sunday 33.
Luke 21:25-28,34-36. Year C, Advent 1.
Luke 22:14-23:56. Year C, Palm Sunday.
Luke 23:35-43. Year C, Christ the King.
Luke 24:1-12, Year C, Easter Vigil.
Luke 24:13-35. Year A, Easter 3.
Luke 24:35-48. Year B, Easter 3.
Luke 24:46-53. Year C, Ascension.

John 1:1-18. Christmas, Day; Second Sunday after Christmas.
John 1:6-8,19-28. Year B, Advent 3.
John 1:29-34. Year A, Sunday 2.
John 1:35-42. Year B, Sunday 2.
John 2:1-11. Year C, Sunday 2.
John 2:13-22. Lateran Basilica.
John 2:13-25. Year B, Lent 3.
John 3:13-17. Triumph of the Cross.
John 3:14-21. Year B, Lent 4.
John 3:16-18. Year A, Trinity.
John 4:5-42. Year A, Lent 3.
John 6:1-15. Year B, Sunday 17.
John 6:24-35. Year B, Sunday 18.
John 6:41-51. Year B, Sunday 19.
John 6:51-58. Year A, Body and Blood of Christ; Year B, Sunday 20.
John 6:60-69. Year B, Sunday 21.
John 7:37-39. Pentecost.
John 8:1-11. Year C, Lent 5.
John 9:1-41. Year A, Lent 4.
John 10:1-10. Year A, Easter 4.
John 10:11-18. Year B, Easter 4.

Acts 10:25-26,34-35,44-48. Year B, Easter 6.
Acts 10:34,37-43. Easter Day.
Acts 10:34-38. Year A, Baptism of the Lord.
Acts 12:1-11. Saints Peter and Paul.
Acts 13:14,43-52. Year C, Easter 4.
Acts 13:16-17,22-25. Christmas, Vigil.
Acts 13:22-26. Birth of John the Baptist.
Acts 13:46-49. Saint Patrick.
Acts 14:21-27. Year C, Easter 5.
Acts 15:1-2,22-29. Year C, Easter 6.

Romans 1:1-7. Year A, Advent 4.
Romans 3:21-25,28. Year A, Sunday 9.
Romans 4:13,16-18,22. Saint Joseph.
Romans 4:18-25. Year A, Sunday 10.
Romans 5:1-2,5-8. Year A, Lent 3.
Romans 5:1-5. Year C, Trinity.
Romans 5:5-11. Year C, Sacred Heart.
Romans 5:6-11. Year A, Sunday 11.
Romans 5:12-15. Year A, Sunday 12.
Romans 5:12-19. Year A, Lent 1.
Romans 6:3-11. Easter Vigil.
Romans 6:3-4,8-11. Year A, Sunday 13.
Romans 8:8-11. Year A, Lent 5.
Romans 8:8-17. Year C, Pentecost.
Romans 8:9,11-13. Year A, Sunday 14.
Romans 8:14-17. Year B, Trinity.
Romans 8:18-23. Year A, Sunday 15.
Romans 8:22-27. Pentecost.
Romans 8:26-27. Year A, Sunday 16.
Romans 8:28-30. Year A, Sunday 17.
Romans 8:31-34. Year B, Lent 2.
Romans 8:35,37-39. Year A, Sunday 18.
Romans 9:1-5. Year A, Sunday 19.
Romans 10:8-13. Year C, Lent 1.
Romans 11:13-15,29-32. Year A, Sunday 20.
Romans 11:33-36. Year A, Sunday 21.
Romans 12:1-2. Year A, Sunday 22.
Romans 13:8-10. Year A, Sunday 23.
Romans 13:11-14. Year A, Advent 1.
Romans 14:7-9. Year A, Sunday 24.
Romans 15:4-9. Year A, Advent 2.
Romans 16:25-27. Year B, Advent 4.

Galatians 1:1-2,6-10. Year C, Sunday 9.
Galatians 1:11-19. Year C, Sunday 10.
Galatians 1:11-20. Saints Peter and Paul.
Galatians 2:16,19-21. Year C, Sunday 11.
Galatians 3:26-29. Year C, Sunday 12.
Galatians 4:4-7. Mary Mother of God.
Galatians 5:1,13-18. Year C, Sunday 13.
Galatians 5:16-25. Year B, Pentecost.
Galatians 6:14-18. Year C, Sunday 14.

Ephesians 1:3-6,11-12. Immaculate Conception.
Ephesians 1:3-6,15-18. Second Sunday after Christmas.
Ephesians 1:3-14. Year B, Sunday 15.
Ephesians 1:17-23. Ascension.
Ephesians 2:4-10. Year B, Lent 4.
Ephesians 2:13-18. Year B, Sunday 16.
Ephesians 3:2-3,5-6. Epiphany.
Ephesians 3:8-12,14-19. Year B, Sacred Heart.
Ephesians 4:1-6. Year B, Sunday 17.
Ephesians 4:1-13. Year B, Ascension.
Ephesians 4:17,20-24. Year B, Sunday 18.
Ephesians 4:30-5:2. Year B, Sunday 19.
Ephesians 5:8-14. Year A, Lent 4.
Ephesians 5:15-20. Year B, Sunday 20.
Ephesians 5:21-32. Year B, Sunday 21.

Philippians 1:3-6,8-11. Year C, Advent 2.
Philippians 1:20-24,27. Year A, Sunday 25.
Philippians 2:1-11. Year A, Sunday 26.
Philippians 2:6-11. Palm Sunday; Triumph of the Cross.
Philippians 3:8-14. Year C, Lent 5.
Philippians 3:17-4:1. Year C, Lent 2.
Philippians 4:4-7. Year C, Advent 3.
Philippians 4:6-9. Year A, Sunday 27.
Philippians 4:12-14,19-20. Year A, Sunday 28.

Colossians 1:12-20. Year C, Christ the King.
Colossians 1:15-20. Year C, Sunday 15.
Colossians 1:24-28. Year C, Sunday 16.
Colossians 2:12-14. Year C, Sunday 17.
Colossians 3:1-4. Easter Day.
Colossians 3:1-5,9-11. Year C, Sunday 18.
Colossians 3:12-21. Year A, Holy Family.

Hebrews 12:1-4. Year C, Sunday 20.
Hebrews 12:5-7,11-13. Year C, Sunday 21.
Hebrews 12:18-19,22-24. Year C, Sunday 22.

James 1:17-18,21-22,27. Year B, Sunday 22.
James 2:1-5. Year B, Sunday 23.
James 2:14-18. Year B, Sunday 24.
James 3:16-4:3. Year B, Sunday 25.
James 5:1-6. Year B, Sunday 26.
James 5:7-10. Year A, Advent 3.

1 Peter 1:3-9. Year A, Easter 2.
1 Peter 1:8-12. Birth of John the Baptist.
1 Peter 1:17-21. Year A, Easter 3.
1 Peter 2:4-9. Year A, Easter 5.
1 Peter 2:20-25. Year A, Easter 4.
1 Peter 3:15-18. Year A, Easter 6.
1 Peter 3:18-22. Year B, Lent 1.
1 Peter 4:13-16. Year A, Easter 7.

2 Peter 1:16-19. Transfiguration.
2 Peter 3:8-14. Year B, Advent 2.

1 John 2:1-5. Year B, Easter 3.
1 John 3:1-2. Year B, Easter 4.
1 John 3:1-2,21-24. Year C, Holy Family.
1 John 3:1-3. All Saints.
1 John 3:18-24. Year B, Easter 5.
1 John 4:7-10. Year B, Easter 6.
1 John 4:7-16. Year A, Sacred Heart.
1 John 4:11-16. Year B, Easter 7.
1 John 5:1-6. Year B, Easter 2.
1 John 5:1-9. Year B, Baptism of the Lord.

Revelation 1:5-8. Year B, Christ the King.
Revelation 1:9-13,17-19. Year C, Easter 2.
Revelation 5:11-14. Year C, Easter 3.
Revelation 7:2-4,9-14. All Saints.
Revelation 7:9,14-17. Year C, Easter 4.
Revelation 11:19; 12:1-6,10. Assumption.
Revelation 21:1-5. Year C, Easter 5.
Revelation 21:10-14,22-23. Year C, Easter 6.
Revelation 22:12-14,16-17,20. Year C, Easter 7.